CONSENSUS IS NOT KUMBAYA

Lessons in Tough-Minded Leadership

RAND GOLLETZ

M·J

NEW YORK

CONSENSUS IS NOT KUMBAYA

Lessons in Tough-Minded Leadership

by RAND GOLLETZ

Library of Congress Control Number: 2010930258
ISBN 978-1-60037-817-1 (paperback)
ISBN 978-1-60037-818-8 (hard cover)

Published by:

MORGAN JAMES PUBLISHING
1225 Franklin Ave. Ste 325
Garden City, NY 11530-1693
Toll Free 800-485-4943
www.MorganJamesPublishing.com

Cover photo by:
Eli Turner
Freed Photography
Bethesda, MD

Interior Design by:
Bonnie Bushman
bbushman@bresnan.net

For Morna, amazing grace

ACKNOWLEDGMENTS

I have always been interested in *power:* who has it, who doesn't, how it's used, how it affects people. I'm especially curious to know why some leaders wield power to benefit others while others do so for their *own* benefit.

Over the past 35 years, I've worked for a few great leaders whose power has benefited multitudes. Unfortunately, many fell into the other category. When I became a C-level leader myself, I promised I'd become a "servant leader" like those I've admired. With pride, I can say I've stayed true to that promise—and I didn't do it alone.

I'm deeply indebted to all of the people and teams who were a part of my corporate leadership journey. All the interactions I've had with people at all levels have enriched my life and propelled my development. If you are one of those people (and you KNOW who you are): Thank you for being a part of my life.

For the last decade, I've been dedicated to helping both aspiring and experienced business leaders define and create success. They have given me far more than I've given them. As anyone in professional services knows, all client experiences are not equally enjoyable, but all of them should be fulfilling. The vast majority of mine have been both. To my valued clients: Thanks for your business, your trust, and your friendship.

My parents instilled traditional values and a "nose-to-the-grindstone" approach to life. Endure no matter what; no free lunch. To them, my love and thanks.

Morna, my wife and partner for more than 30 years, has consistently supported my successes, encouraged me when I've failed, and stood by me when I've "shot myself in the foot." To Morna: You're simply the best.

On to this book. When Peter Schnall, my client and friend, agreed to write the Foreword, I'm sure he had no idea what he'd signed up for. He's one of the smartest and most capable people I know. But beyond that, the commitment he has to his development and evolution as a man and a great leader is as clear in his Foreword as it is in our work together. To Peter: I'm grateful for your time, patience, and flexibility.

To Rob Ryan and Eric Schweikert, men of exceptional character I'm proud to call friends: Many thanks for your back-cover endorsements.

There is no escaping that this book would never have made it to print without Barbara McNichol, editor, sounding board, and taskmaster. Given my finite attention span, many times during our review and rewrite process I had "had enough." Barbara cajoled and prodded me, knowing "when to hold 'em and when to fold 'em." I'm certain she has had psychotherapeutic training but won't acknowledge as much. To Barbara: I'm grateful for your contribution and especially for never compromising my "voice" amid all of the changes we made.

The people at Morgan James publish about 5% of the manuscripts they receive. Somehow, I made it through their rigorous triage course. To David Hancock, Robyn Spizman, Lyza Poulin, and the creative, production, and administrative teams at M-J: Thank you for your "tough love" throughout the publishing process.

Foreword

A number of years ago, an executive coach told me that my only job was to clone myself. I thought that was crazy; my job was to make decisions, make things happen, drive change.

I argued; she held her ground; we called it a day, and I went home to sleep on the debate. The next morning, I resolved to give her crazy cloning idea a try and cast every action as an opportunity to teach my colleagues how I think, how I decide, and how I move ideas forward.

After that, every meeting became a teaching moment. I asked deeper questions and explained why I was asking. And if I had to decide, I explained *why* I was deciding—what my logic said and what my heart was telling me.

This new approach was a revelation, a through-the-red-sea moment. Guided by faith, I took a step into forbidding waters that, to my amazement, parted and gave me entrance into a new world. I have forged a career marked by through-the-red-sea moments of discovery.

That's not to say I became a master all at once or even that I am one today. It is to say my coach provoked me to look at my leadership agenda in a radically new way that made me a better executive.

My leadership development journey began just months into my first job after college. An early boss told me I should think in graphs rather than in equations. That may never have been your leadership issue, but I think you'll recognize my emotional response: I thought, "What right does anyone have to tell me how to think!"

But I also saw how much more compelling his explanations were than mine and decided to give it a shot. I set out deliberately not only to change my presentations, but also to change my work process that led up to them. I got faster, made fewer mistakes, and got better at explaining to my boss what I had done—my first trip through-the-red-sea.

Some reinventions are essentially simple; others meet stubborn resistance from personal demons, habits, and insecurities. The most hurtful, accurate, and still frustratingly in need of attention showed up in these two words on a performance appraisal in the early '90s: "Be Humble." Damn, that one has been hard.

Since then, I've had a commitment to humility *in my head* that has been difficult to turn into an automatic reflex *in my heart.* I'm still trying to get through-the-red-sea on that one.

Rand and I first met when he was coaching a colleague. Like all good coaches, he observes carefully, reads broadly, and is always ready with a framework.

Unlike most coaches, Rand has "been there and done that." Having been a top executive, he knows firsthand what it takes to lead an organization—how to deal with both talented and difficult subordinates, make music with a challenging boss, and drive results year after year.

He is also restless without being unnecessarily impatient and tough-minded without being hard-headed. Rand delivers a powerful combination of solid pedagogy, battle-tested principles, and empathetic deep wisdom.

And he can provoke those through-the-red-sea moments—which is my greatest tribute to a coach.

Here's an example. Once at dinner, I expressed frustration that I wasn't able to fulfill all my vision for the company. Rand asked, "Do you feel that you personally have to solve all of the company's problems?"

"Well, of course not," said my head. My heart wasn't quite there yet—and off I went through-the-red-sea, with his help, to reinvent my understanding of how I could trust my talented colleagues to work with me in building a better company.

You'll find that *Consensus is Not Kumbaya* depicts Rand perfectly. When you read his words, it's the same as hearing them in person. Either way, he is challenging, direct, and principled—and he is wise, pragmatic, and understanding. All that said, as his client and friend, maybe the thing I value most about Rand is this: For him, "truth" is more important than "comfort."

In his approach, he first demands debate and discovery of principles. Then he provides step-by-step advice, but with a challenge: If you don't adopt the right attitude, you will make only incremental change—and that just isn't good enough.

I read this book as an invitation to go through-the-red-sea into a new, uncomfortable world without excuses. Rand challenges the conventional mindset of what executive leadership is about, gives you a roadmap, and urges you to start your journey. It's a provocative gift.

Good luck and bon voyage!

Peter Schnall
Chief Risk Officer
Capital One Financial Corporation

Introduction

Welcome to a journey into the mind of an unconventional thinker.

For my entire career as a "C" level leader, consultant, and executive coach, I've been intrigued and perplexed by the arbitrary distinctions that so-called "experts" have drawn between management and leadership.

For some, management is a set of disciplines—primarily planning, organizing, staffing, and controlling—and leadership is a way of engaging and communicating that wins them followers. While both the technical and interpersonal aspects of effective stewardship are important, I don't make arbitrary "leadership versus management" distinctions because together they form the capabilities required for success.

Here's where I DO make a distinction—and why I believe you should read this book.

During the last 25 (or so) years, purveyors of the "kumbaya" view of the world have proffered the belief that effective leaders must be warm and cuddly. Conversely, proponents of the "tough-as-nails" view of leadership have countered that belief with one of their own—that tough-minded leadership, in practice, must look like what I would call hard-headed leadership to be effective.

In my view, neither of those propositions is accurate. Rather than being a "black and white" proposition, *leadership* exists mostly in shades of gray. That said, my intention with this book is to convince you of the following:

- Mental toughness is a requirement for successful leadership.
- Tough-minded leaders are neither purveyors of "kumbaya" nor those with hard-headed traits.
- Tough-minded leadership is best understood by viewing it through the lens of real-life examples in action.
- You can and will become more effective by applying the real-life lessons in tough-minded leadership you find here.
- Because you're always looking to leverage your pressure-filled time, a book needs to provoke you, needle you, entertain you, and humor you as well as inform you to capture and hold your attention.

I've led organizations large and small. I've run profit centers and staff groups. I've been a CEO and a COO as well as the Chief Marketing Officer of a Fortune 500 company. I've also led a large consulting practice.

Currently, as principal of my company, I work with senior Fortune 500 executives as well as entrepreneurs to propel their success. For 30 years, I have used all of my professional pursuits as laboratories to test my own leadership insights as well as the insights of others. My experience and disposition enable me to counsel edgy, eager executives seeking a trusted advisor who has "been there and done that."

That's what I do. And I love what I do.

As part of my support to them, I stay abreast of current leadership thinking by reading business books. Being restless and impatient, I find much of the literature to be intentionally or unintentionally complex, derivative, self-indulgent, or boring. Not wanting to fall into the "sameness" trap, I resisted publishing a book of my own until I could overcome that possibility.

After writing *Consensus is Not Kumbaya*, I believe I have succeeded. You'll find that every brief chapter has been distilled from my direct experience as an executive, consultant, or coach. Conveying what has worked and what has not, each lesson addresses "C" suite priorities and delivers ideas that merit consideration.

Please regard *Consensus is Not Kumbaya* as a book you'll place on your night table and read one short chapter each night before lights-out. Then from that one concise, digestible lesson, you'll take one relevant action the very next day. If you do this, things will change. I promise.

Begin this book anywhere. The chapters are organized arbitrarily, so don't let my structure impose order on your reading. Both chapter order and titles aim to stimulate your interest, not regulate it. Think of this as a book of essays. With a couple of exceptions, each one is a "stand-alone."

Those who know me call my worldview "skeptical." Perhaps it comes from my early career working with and for executives who were more obsessed with *looking* good than *doing* good. I watched many wield power for their own benefit—or just because they could.

Today, I believe down to my socks that any legitimate exercise of power must benefit others. In that regard, I've gained a lot from working with extraordinary "servant leaders." The lessons in this book point you toward achieving that end, too, with healthy doses of sarcasm, skepticism, and humor built in.

An old adage asks: "If a tree falls in the forest and no one is around to hear it, did it make a sound?" My analogous question is: "If ideas and solutions are proposed in a business book, yet no one reads it or implements them, was the book worth writing?" My answer is a resounding "NO!"

So spend a few minutes each day reading *Consensus is Not Kumbaya.* Think about its lessons, implement its ideas, and take tough-minded leadership to the next level in your organization.

Rand Golletz

Examples from sports reinforce how the "inner game" trumps the "outer game." Tough-minded leaders get real, get tough, and get going.

What Does Tough-Minded Really Mean?

To create success, you have to be tough-minded. But what does that mean?

Let me explain by way of example. My wife's second cousin Ansley Cargill has been one great tennis player. As a freshman at Duke, she finished the year as second-ranked NCAA player and a first-team all-American. Impressive! At the same time, she carried an equally impressive GPA of 3.8. Then she left college after her freshman year to join the pro tennis tour. That's when she confronted reality head-on. She played in major events and even beat a few highly ranked players, lifting her own ranking into the 70s. (In fact, she played Venus Williams more than once, even in the U.S. Open—a humbling experience.)

Watching Ansley play in college, she looked like a world beater as she decimated her opponents. But when she turned pro (and ranking in the 70s says "you are a P-L-A-Y-E-R"), she faced athletes highly prepared for the big time. Her situation conjures up a scene from the movie *The Natural* when Roy Hobbs (Robert

Redford) had just struck out in his first major league at bat and the voice on the PA system said, "Welcome to the majors, Mr. Hobbs."

Ansley noted that the difference in physical ability among the top 100 players was insignificant; the major difference of those consistently in the top 10 was their ability to be totally "in the moment." They could instantly shut out the last point like finished business and focus on the next. No past, no future, right there 100%. That defines tough-mindedness in action. (To let you know, Ansley decided pro tennis wasn't for her. She left the tour, graduated from Duke, and works in business today.)

Despite his recent off-the-course problems, golfer Tiger Woods is a tough-minded athlete.

Golf coach Butch Harmon said that Tiger's father, Earl Woods, was a great golf coach, maybe the greatest golf coach in history. Although not a great golfer himself, Earl had been in the U.S. military, the Green Berets. When Tiger was learning to play golf before the age of 10, his dad created a multitude of exercises to teach him mental toughness. At the same time, his mom taught him the concepts of Buddhism and meditation to help him create mental mastery. These first teachers showed Tiger how to mentally rehearse using imagery to build confidence, and not get distracted by dropping clubs, coughing, or other interruptions.

One spring, San Francisco 49ers head coach Mike Singletary brought a new kind (and new level) of pain to his team's training camp. Known simply as "the hill," it's a 45-degree incline that he had built for running. Singletary first witnessed the use of hill running during his time as a Hall of Fame middle linebacker with the 1980s Chicago Bears. While it obviously increased players' endurance, its primary benefit was a significant increase in players' persistence and perseverance. Walter Payton, Singletary's 1980s teammate and the Bears record-setting running back, believed that hill running helped players overcome the mental obstacles that get in the way of success. Many people still believe the 1985 Bears was the best NFL team in history. Almost all of the so-called "experts" still believe they were the toughest.

Dave Goggins is a Navy SEAL living in Chula Vista, California. He joined the Navy as a 240-pound power-lifter. SEAL training began his journey to well-rounded fitness. He subsequently ran marathons, ultramarathons, and (later) triathlons. He also completed the Ultraman—a megatriathlon that features a grueling combination of a 6.2-mile ocean swim, a 261-mile bike ride, and a 52.4-mile run. Dave does this ostensibly to raise money for the Special Ops Warrior Foundation (SOWF). But people who know him insist that if SOWF didn't exist, he'd find another reason to compete.

Dave believes that with focus and discipline, anyone can do just about anything. "I want to see if there is a limit to the human soul," Goggins says. His motto is "show no weakness." He visualizes success before undertaking any significant challenge and adds the following: "I remember when I was younger, when things were really hard or difficult, they could be so hard that they made you want to quit. That's a feeling I'll never have again." Dave is one of the toughest guys walking the face of the earth.

These examples reinforce how the "inner game" trumps the "outer game." Tough-minded leaders get real, get tough, and get going. Among their attributes:

- They strive for objectivity, making distinctions among facts, intuition, guesswork, and wishful thinking. (That's getting real.)

- They have the ability, inclination, and discipline to face any situation with strength, resolve, and equanimity. Discipline, the key word here, is defined as "doing what needs to be done, when it needs to be done, the way it needs to be done, every time." It presupposes delaying gratification and doing the hard work first. (That's getting tough.)
- They understand that a good decision executed today is better than a perfect decision executed in six months. (That's getting going.)

What attributes do you have that show your tough-mindedness? In what ways do you get real, get tough, and get going?

"Tough-minded managers know their job is to get people to want to do *what needs to be done; hard-headed managers are satisfied merely getting people to* do *what needs to be done."*

Want Success? Discard Hard-Headedness for Tough-Mindedness

Several characteristics distinguish "tough-minded" leadership from "hard-headed" management practices. Consider these:

- Tough-minded execs pursue action that achieves planned results; hard-headed managers aim to solidify their authority and personal power.
- Tough-minded execs select people for jobs based on past performance and position-relevant strengths; hard-headed ones hire people whose views and perspectives match their own.
- Tough-minded managers select strong people and integrate those strengths to create interdependent success; hard-headed managers select weak people, aim to develop their weaknesses, and end up cultivating their dependency.
- Tough-minded managers show a committed candor in their interactions; hard-headed managers verbally espouse a commitment to candor, but "shoot the messenger" when they don't like the news.

- Tough-minded execs encourage a constant flow of people, from all organizational levels, in and out of their offices; hard-headed ones believe that an "open-door policy" means leaving their doors open and waiting for people to come in.
- Tough-minded execs nurture commitment; hard-headed ones mandate obedience.
- Tough-minded execs recognize that giving people a say doesn't necessarily mean giving them a vote; hard-headed ones don't acknowledge the difference. (They don't even bother to think about it.)
- Tough-minded execs understand that their primary lever of superior organizational performance is people, both customers and associates, so they spend the highest proportion of their time with people; hard-headed ones view any time spent with people as a costly distraction.
- Tough-minded execs use personal interactions as coaching opportunities; hard-headed ones use them to demonstrate personal bravado.
- Tough-minded execs understand that time is their most precious resource and learn to manage it well; hard-headed ones allow time to manage them.
- Tough-minded execs know how to sustain individual and organizational performance; hard-headed ones may "get it" for a short time, but rarely "get it" consistently over time.
- Tough-minded managers know their job is to get people to *want to do* what needs to be done; hard-headed managers are satisfied merely getting people to *do* what needs to be done.

Review these characteristics again with candor and then look in the mirror. Which ones characterize you?

Words create images and stories in our minds about people and situations. Effective "leadership" is about the quality of our conversations, the images that they create, and the actions that they compel. Yet here we sit using a word like "consensus" without agreement on what it means.

Consensus is Not Kumbaya!

My client Frank (not his real name) had just been elected chairman and CEO. His promotion was wildly popular and widely celebrated. His company, a Fortune 500 firm with more than 100,000 associates and 80 operating divisions worldwide, had elected only eight chairmen in its 100-year history. All had been life-long associates. The company had a history of ascending growth and earnings and a stable corporate culture, including corporate values that management both talked and walked. From an investor's point of view, this was a "buy-and-hold" stock.

At the time of his election, Frank was 55 years old. Until his early 40s, his career was successful but unspectacular. No one really pegged him as "the guy" until the chairman at the time put him in charge of the firm's largest division. There, he hit a home run; actually, he became Babe Ruth. To continue the baseball analogy, he led the league in home runs for the next decade, was made vice chairman at the age of 53, and placed in a head-to-head "competition" for the top job with the impressive president and COO.

Tough-minded without being hard-headed, Frank has five distinct strengths. He's gifted at selecting and developing associates. He communicates extremely well with people from all walks of life. He's an incredible listener, enveloping people with his attention. He also "connects the dots." In corporate parlance, it's called integrative thinking. His biggest strength, however, is his self-knowledge. Acutely aware of his strengths and weaknesses—personal as well as professional—he has never dismissed his shortcomings as irrelevant or unimportant. He creates "work-arounds" to compensate.

Before Frank became chairman, he had a reputation as a great collaborator. He recognized the importance of winning emotional commitment from people and worked hard to obtain it.

In his first several months as chairman and mine as his executive coach, Frank asked me to attend his regularly scheduled staff meetings. I had been working with him for some time, and the company's senior leaders knew and trusted me. I had become his "eyes and ears" in the company and had a reputation as a guy who acted responsibly and confidentially with what I saw and heard. One Monday morning during a meeting break, Jake, the president of the company's largest operating group, approached me with a concerned look. Our brief discussion went something like this:

Jake: "Rand, do you sense something different about Frank since he became chairman?"

Me: "What do you mean 'different'? He's now the chairman; I'd say that's pretty different. You guys are trying hard to relate to him in a new way because of his role. That's also different. The power dynamic in the group has changed. That's also something different. So yes, I sense that EVERYTHING has changed, and yes, it's different."

Jake: "I realize that stuff, Rand. I'm not talking about that. What I mean is, Frank seems to have become an autocrat. I feel like asking him, 'Hey, who are you, and what did you do with Frank?' It seems like he's imposing his will because he CAN—even when situations don't require it. We talked in our last meeting together about the priority of 'consensus.' He always seemed diligent in the past about 'walking the talk.' Not so much now!"

Me: "I'll think about your comments. Let's revisit this issue."

Subsequently, other members of the senior leadership team called me and expressed a similar concern. I asked Frank if we could discuss this at his next staff meeting. His response: "Fine, as long as it doesn't become a whining session."

Here's what happened.

After they covered their normal business, I mentioned that several people on the team had brought up an apparent change in Frank's management style. I then asked that each of them pull out a piece of paper and write the word "consensus." A few of them rolled their eyes and I thought, "If this goes poorly, I'm outta here!"

I asked them to write a definition of that word and hand it to me. They did. I then collected and read the definitions, without attribution. They differed greatly. For some of them, consensus had something to do with voting before deciding. For a few, it had to do with reaching unanimity before executing major decisions. Still others had different ideas.

To a person, they gazed at me with looks that I interpreted as meaning, "OK, big shot. Why should I give a damn about any of this? You're wasting my valuable time."

I gulped and continued, "When I spoke to each of you individually about Frank and his style, you all used shorthand to express your thoughts. I heard the word 'empowerment' eight times. I heard the word 'delegation' just as often. Several of you used the word 'autocrat.' The word I heard most often was 'consensus.' Each of you used those words as if we should—or DID—automatically agree on what they meant.

"Here's my point: Words create images and stories in our minds about people and situations. Effective 'leadership' is about the quality of our conversations, the images that they create, and the actions that they compel. Yet here we sit using a word like 'consensus' without agreement on what it means."

I saw light bulbs go on, so I summarized, "It might seem frivolous on the surface, but I think we need to agree that on key issues, you need to have a way of getting to your assumptions about what things mean, so that you're not taking inconsistent action and operating with divergent assumptions."

To start, we spent two hours—*two hours*—on what the word "consensus" would mean to the team going forward. Here's what we concluded: Consensus would mean that before action would be taken on issues above a certain threshold, all team members could and would *support* the decision, even if they didn't believe it was the *best* possible decision. Consensus would not imply *how* a decision would be reached. Some decisions would still be made by Frank—alone with no input. Some would be voted on. Some would be debated in advance. Some would not. The point is, consensus would not imply the decision-making process employed; it merely would imply whether active support for a decision existed. In this case, whether their definition comported with Webster's definition was less important than their recognition that common understanding was critical.

What are the implications for you? Never, ever, ever assume that you and your team are on the same page unless you've tested for understanding, debated issues, worked hard to surface objections, and considered alternatives. Agreement isn't always necessary and consensus isn't about creating a "kumbaya" management approach.

Dialogue presents the best route to mutual understanding, conviction, energy, development, and commitment. It's not, as some would cynically speculate, the route to terminal niceness; rather, it propels the sustained achievement of results.

The Rewards of Dialoguing Well

Leadership is a conversation. If the purpose of leadership is to institutionalize change and influence those who must execute it, then ultimately leaders must influence both individuals and teams to want to do what needs to be done.

The key word here is *want.* Case in point: When I was a young college graduate, one of my first bosses was a guy who managed by fear and intimidation. He was extremely adept at getting associates to do what needed to be done, but the only *want* involved was us *wanting* to keep our jobs.

Look at the top arrow in the diagram on page 24. It illustrates the point that while leadership is a conversation, those conversations conducted by business leaders vary in type and quality. (Thanks to Noel Tichy and Peter Senge for some of the ideas expressed in this diagram.)

Approaches to Leadership Conversation

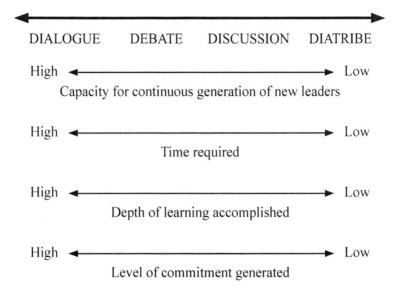

DIALOGUE DEBATE DISCUSSION DIATRIBE

High ← → Low
Capacity for continuous generation of new leaders

High ← → Low
Time required

High ← → Low
Depth of learning accomplished

High ← → Low
Level of commitment generated

Many leaders try to influence others with **diatribes.** Those are mind-numbing monologues intended to transmit a demand for action in as little time and with as little discourse as possible. Diatribes occasionally include some contrived "win-one-for-the-Gipper" language, as well. If you were looking through a glass wall at a diatribe, one party (typically the one with more power or authority) would be doing all of the talking and the others would be doing all of the listening.

Moving across the continuum, the next form of conversation is **discussion.** In a typical business discussion, the parties bring their preconceptions and points of view to an exchange that often, but not always, turns out to be unproductive. Most of the time, the intention is not to change minds or resolve a problem, but only to express opinions.

At the end of a business **debate,** on the other hand, presumably a decision is reached. However, while debates frequently result in decisions, they often create win-lose outcomes that don't engender enthusiastic support.

A **dialogue** is the most robust and fruitful form of conversation. It creates a "pool of shared meaning." It also requires engaged listening. Many managerial leaders invoke listening only so they can catch their breath before resuming their diatribe. Dialogue creates an understanding of context, perspective, and insight as well as content.

Effective leaders recognize the key points provided in the diagram. First, a part of managerial leadership—maybe the most important part—consists of developing future leaders. Second, learning by all parties ought to be an outcome of leadership conversation. Third, while the time required may be considerable, it's a small cost considering the substantial benefits. Fourth, dialogue gives you the best opportunity to gain commitment to ideas and initiatives.

Look at the bottom arrow on the diagram. If your organization requires positive energy and voluntary contribution rather than obedience, where do you need to be on the scale from diatribe to dialogue?

Remember, obedience may get you to this quarter's financial targets, but it won't get you to the promised land!

Dialogue presents the best route to mutual understanding, conviction, energy, development, and commitment. It's not, as some would cynically speculate, the route to terminal niceness; rather, it propels the sustained achievement of results.

It's time for political correctness to take a back seat to the truth. Many who have not accomplished the degree of financial success that others have achieved have failed by choice. The unconscious choices they've made may have been fueled by inertia, but they're still choices. So are inaction, blaming, and staying stuck.

Your Good Fortune is a Matter of Choice, Not Chance

Back in 2000 during the U.S. election campaign, a presidential aspirant said in a speech about income taxes, "Those who have been lucky at the gaming table of life should be forced to share their winnings with those who have been less fortunate." Does that mean this candidate, Dick Gephardt, compares life to a roulette wheel with prosperity coming through chance? What a crock!

Gephardt's message implies that if you've been financially successful, you should feel lucky, undeserving, or guilty. Apparently you achieved your success with smoke and mirrors.

Conversely, if you haven't achieved a level of prosperity, it's not your fault. Those who have achieved financial success ordained your fate, supposedly attaining success at your expense. What a crock times two!!

I know a guy who, like me, has earned a substantial sum in his life, but today has nothing to show for it—he spent it all. Under current U.S. law, this guy will be taxed in retirement at a lower rate than I will because his money (or lack thereof) will be earning much less money than mine. He believes that's fair; I believe he should move to Cuba.

Of course, some people face difficult circumstances and need assistance. I know that. Here's my point: *It's time for political correctness to take a back seat to the truth.* Many who have not achieved the degree of financial success that you've achieved have failed by choice. The unconscious choices they've made may have been fueled by inertia, but they're still choices. So are inaction, blaming, and staying stuck.

Financially successful business leaders have also made a choice—to be engaged in creating prosperity. Their attributes of hard work, risk taking, and initiative should be admired and cultivated. Blame, victimization, irresponsibility, excuse making, and lack of ambition should not. As the late business philosopher Jim Rohn once speculated, "If you took all of the money in this country away from everyone today and distributed it equally among the entire population of adults, within five years it would be distributed in the same proportions that it was before you took it."

Where does being "fortunate" fit into *that* equation?

"Our attitudes about money, power, politics, personal relationships, and self-esteem all develop durable foundations before we reach age ten! What gets stuffed into our subconscious minds forms the basis for our governing beliefs."

Your Truth vs. "The" Truth

In the 1988 movie *Bull Durham*, Crash Davis, played by Kevin Costner, relayed his most deeply held beliefs to Annie Savoy, played by Susan Sarandon. Here's the dialogue, with a few words omitted for the sake of decency:

"Well, I believe in the soul . . . the small of a woman's back, the hanging curve ball, high fiber, good scotch, and that the novels of Susan Sontag are self-indulgent, overrated crap. I believe Lee Harvey Oswald acted alone. I believe there ought to be a constitutional amendment outlawing AstroTurf and the designated hitter. I believe in the sweet spot, soft-core pornography, opening presents Christmas morning rather than Christmas Eve, and I believe in long, slow, deep, soft, wet kisses that last three days." Savoy responded with a breathy, "Oh my!"

Those are Davis's beliefs. To a large degree, our lives are directed or governed by beliefs, too. When I introduce this notion and its consequences to my clients, they tend to respond, not with a breathy "Oh my!" but with two of the most dangerous words in the English language: "I know!" Our discussions reveal that what

"I know" really means is "I understand, abstractly, what you mean, but I don't exactly understand the implications for me, although I see it in other people all the time."

Implications of How the Mind Works

What follows is a brief tutorial on how the human mind functions, why that is, what it implies for effective behavior, and what you can do about it. Hang in here with my explanation; it will be worth your while.

At birth and then for the first six to eight years of life, we humans have not yet developed a conscious mind, the part that reasons and can accept or reject information. The subconscious part of the mind accepts everything as true. So, for the first six to eight years of life, primary influencers—parents, siblings, teachers—have proffered extraordinary, unchallenged influence. If, for example, we witnessed our parents constantly fighting in those six to eight years, that's probably how we'd perceive the state of marriage. Its implications can persist the rest of our lives.

Similarly, our attitudes about money, power, politics, personal relationships, and self-esteem all develop durable foundations before we reach age ten! What gets stuffed into our subconscious minds forms the basis for our governing beliefs (also referred to as our worldview, our truth, our map).

Here's what happened in my first eight years. I grew up in a blue-collar, 1950s home where money was tight. My parents held basic attitudes about wealth and rich people; that is, some people had money, others didn't—depends on the luck of the draw. I remember frequently hearing this expression: "Those who have, get," implying that the rich get richer and the poor get poorer. It also implied that financial success had more to do with luck and little to do with effort. That message lingers with me to this day. Now that I understand it, I don't buy into it, but still, that message reverberates in my psyche: "Those who have, get."

It's an obstacle to financial success that I have to call out and overcome when it whispers in my ear. What phrases—and obstacles—keep calling out to you?

Unless you consciously reprogram your mental chatter, it will validate and reinforce your governing beliefs—and keep you stuck in place your entire life!

Beliefs Versus Truth—Beware the Difference

The seeds of everything that's possible for you were planted in your pre-adolescent years. Those seeds take in fresh water every time you dismiss or degrade ideas that contradict them, or when you treat them as "the truth" rather than your beliefs when they arise.

You say, "I don't do that!" Oh, really! Then try on the following questions for size:

- If you are a political liberal, when was the last time you read something by conservative columnists George Will or David Brooks? Are you open to the notion that you might learn something valuable by doing so?
- If you're a fiscal conservative, does your library include the writings of economist John Kenneth Galbraith as a counterpoint to those of economist Milton Friedman?
- Do you "hang" on the words of conservative broadcaster Bill O'Reilly or liberal broadcaster Keith Olbermann as if they're unbiased and completely objective?

- Do you require approval before implementing new initiatives at work? Do you automatically defer to the "higher-ups" in your organization?

The biases represented by your answers to those questions began developing during your pre-adolescence. As you grew older, they were exacerbated by what Dr. Srikumar Rao of the London Business School calls your "mental chatter."

Let's face it. Mental chatter sticks with you. It starts in the morning when you awake, continues all day, and occasionally keeps you awake at night. It assesses, evaluates, and judges. It prods you to worry about what's coming tomorrow and lament over what happened yesterday. It convinces you that your boss doesn't like you because he didn't respond to your cheerful "hello" at the elevator this morning. Unless you consciously reprogram your mental chatter, it will validate and reinforce your governing beliefs—and keep you stuck your entire life!

Let's take this concept two steps further.

Step number one: Because your psyche is programmed to keep you comfortable, you're not challenged to expand into uncomfortable places. As a matter of fact, your psyche *resists* your traveling to uncomfortable places. Now, the more progress you make challenging your thinking and the closer you get to making actual headway, the more resistance you'll feel.

If you're like most people, you stop short of achieving a goal because that's where you feel the most pain. My friend David Neagle calls this place "the abyss." It describes where you are when you've confronted your unproductive beliefs and thoughts but still haven't adopted new ones to help you achieve your goal. Unless you can crash through this nowhere land, you'll get nowhere, man.

Worse, you'll return to where you were with vigor and conviction, and stay there with redoubled resistance.

The difficulty in moving through the abyss is the challenge you must surmount. So it's critical for you to guard the gates of your mind, allowing in only what will propel you toward who you want to be and where you want to go. All this takes patience, resilience, and perseverance to develop the practice and achieve desired results.

Step number two: As human beings, we aren't rational; we're emotional. We use reason to make sense of our emotions, and yet we take actions based on emotions, not reason. Take a look at the following illustration.

When an event occurs, each of us has a tendency to collapse what actually happens with our story about what happens. Our story is the result of the unconscious, automatic confluence of our governing beliefs, our mental chatter, and our feelings. The resulting judgment becomes "our" truth but it's probably not "the" truth.

How can you begin to see all of this at work and grow more deeply toward "the" truth? Be easy on yourself—it's a lifelong process. If you suffer from the "gotta get results within 24 hours or I'll quit" syndrome or "I keep checking my Blackberry because the world can't get along without me" delusion, you'll find the following exercises especially difficult:

- For one week, once an hour (this is easier if your watch has an alarm), stop what you're doing and ask, "What is my mental chatter telling me about what's going on right now?" (You have to do this frequently and in real time because your self-talk evaporates as quickly as it appears.) As you're doing this, ask,

"What's the genesis of my assessments and observations? Is it possible that my conclusions are a product of my story about what's going on more than what's really going on?"

- If you are a parent, you're wise not to imbue your children with the same judgments you have. (After all, much of it is your story.) Your job is to cultivate their curiosity and help them reach—and then be comfortable questioning—their own conclusions about everything—forever!
- Read information that runs contrary to your own worldview and question, *really* question, whether it might contain a morsel of valid information.
- Examine ways in which your political views (just to pick an obvious one) are extrapolated from your parents' views.
- Watch and read a lot less mass media news. It purports to be objective; it's not. Stay away completely from cable news unless you want to raise your blood pressure.
- Get rid of the people in your life who fit into these categories: naysayers, doomsdayers, dream-slayers, game-players. (Personally, I still have a lot of work to do on the game-playing one, but I'm much further along than I was a decade ago.)
- Examine your "victim stories"—instances in which you believe your demise or failure were caused by the actions of others. (For more on this, see "Wake Up! Evict Your Inner Victim," which follows.) Is this belief a trend? If so, what's the cause of this trend? Dig deep to figure out whether your plight was caused exclusively by others or whether you were an unindicted co-conspirator in your own defeat. Even if you believe you have had no complicity, ask this question: "Is there a way out other than the way in?" If you believe that external

circumstances have to change before you can be successful, YOU ARE SCREWED (and wrong)!

Remember, your success depends on getting closer to "the" truth.

Whiners and victims are psychic vampires who can suck the life out of any room they enter and suck the energy out of the people in it. So stay away from these people. Instead, seek out members of the I am Responsible and Accountable for Everything in My Life Association. Their motto: "No excuses, ever!"

Wake Up! Evict Your Inner Victim

Whenever I discuss my perspective on victim hood with others, it stimulates lots of "but what about" questions. "But what about the holocaust?" "But what about Cambodia in the '70s?" You get the idea. My retort to them is always the same; their reaction to my retort is always the same; the ensuing discussion is always the same. An abbreviated version goes something like this.

Them: "So, Rand, you take a dim view of victim hood. Aren't there some extreme examples in which people are really victimized?"

Me: "Of course the recipients of torture and genocide are victimized. On a less destructive level, every person gets taken advantage of at one time or another. There's a huge difference, however, in being the recipient of treatment intended to victimize on the one hand, and regarding oneself as a victim on the other."

Them: "I don't get it."

Me: "Some people, I'd say *many* people, marinate in a cauldron of psychic dysfunction. They whine about the world and complain about how 'put-upon' others make them feel. They continually, boringly, and irritatingly place the blame for their circumstances on everyone but themselves. And at some level, they like it! Here's a sampling of what they say: 'My boss is a jerk so I can't get promoted; my parents didn't love me, so naturally I have no self-esteem; if that bartender hadn't served me that tenth drink, I wouldn't have hit that school bus; if the burger joint would only cut out the trans fats, I wouldn't weigh four hundred pounds; my business wouldn't have gone bankrupt if it hadn't been for one or more of the following: regulation, competition, legislation, prices, Bangalore, third-world slave shops, recessions, expansions, sinus headaches, male pattern baldness, the full moon, etc.'"

Laying the Foundation for Victim Hood

While some of those assertions may have a modicum of truth in them, these people lay (and re-lay and re-lay) the foundation for living as victims. How? In three ways: (1) They define themselves as victims, automatically implying that someone or something has imprisoned them. It follows that they can't escape from that prison; they must wait until they're freed by that someone or something. What an elegant scam! They can stay stuck forever without taking action because, in their minds, action would be fruitless. Then they can complain forever because their (so-called) victimizer does nothing to relieve their misery. (2) They imply that their misery makes them unique. My response? "C'mon! Every human being has to deal with 'stuff.' But it's not your 'stuff' that determines your success. It's what you do about your 'stuff' that determines your success. Get over yourself!" (3) Many victims take on a recruiting mission to geometrically increase the membership of their two clubs: The Loyal Order of Irritating, Recreational Whining Victims of America, and its sister organization The Submissive, Indulgent Enablers of the Loyal Order of Irritating, Recreational Whining

Victims of America. The former group retains the services of personal injury lawyers ready to extract large sums of money from those they believe are to blame for their malaise—everyone but *themselves*. Members of the latter group (the farm team for the first group) listen and bob their heads in agreement as those victims whine. Both clubs meet at the water coolers and in the restrooms of leading organizations.

Here's the bottom line: Whiners and victims are psychic vampires who can suck the life out of any room they enter and suck the energy out of the people in it. So stay away from these people. Instead, seek out members of the I am Responsible and Accountable for Everything in My Life Association. Their motto: "No excuses, ever!"

Overcoming Victim Hood

With this attitude, I'm not implying you can control *all* of the outcomes in your life. But I do believe the following without equivocation:

- Blame, excuses, and victim hood are toxic, divisive, and diversionary.
- Most people can influence their outcomes to a far greater degree than they do.
- Personal accountability stimulates better planning and execution, both in business and in other arenas of life. It also compels reflection—a prerequisite for developing wisdom.

Remember this: Whatever you think, believe, feel, and act will come to be; it's a four-bagger in baseball parlance. So if you dwell on the inherent unfairness of the universe and the bad deals in your life, wake up! You can't become effective and feel fulfilled if you blame others for your circumstances—ever!

When you create a high level of openness,
you inherit a responsibility for what you do
(and even more importantly, don't *do)*
with what you learn from talking with people.
You have to listen, but you can't overreact.

Don't Let Common Lies Grab Hold

My stated mission is "helping business leaders discover and achieve their potential." Why do I believe this is needed? Because many business leaders (more than half, in my experience) limit their success by failing to give adequate attention to reflection and self-examination.

More than that, they presume their success, past and current, predetermines their success in the future. That spells deep trouble! Those who sustain continuing success are those who balance their rightfully earned confidence with a healthy dose of "Oh my God, what do I do next?" suspicion of their own potential—in large enough doses to keep them honest, reasonably objective, and appropriately paranoid.

Yet, as the Bard would say, "Herein lies the rub." The greater your current success and the higher your perch, the greater the likelihood you're headed for a fall because of the deceptions your mind feeds you. In the spirit of directness, let's look at common lies that play a role in holding back executive success—and overturn them.

THE LIE: "I'm successful because I am intelligent, insightful, and competent about all things. If my critics were as capable as me, they'd be just as successful. But because they're not . . ."

THE TRUTH (as I encourage my clients to see it): You got where you are because of your assets and in spite of your liabilities. You often find that attributes once comprising the strengths required for previous success may now be the liabilities keeping you from future success. An example: Early success came because it required sharp strategic and analytic skills, two of your strengths. But now, you run a more mature enterprise that requires superior operating management skills. If your inner voice keeps providing rationale for a status quo that's outlived its usefulness, you and your organization are headed for deep yogurt.

THE LIE: "Every personal exchange, whether in one-on-one discussions or in meetings, must give participants an 'aha' moment. Moreover, my profound comments must demonstrate that I am omniscient, that I have command of all of the relevant dimensions of the business, and that I am 'the man.'"

THE TRUTH: Get over yourself! First, sitting in an executive chair means you get paid to ask great questions, not to have all of the answers. Do you want to have lasting impact? Then the next time you critique a presentation, instead of saying, "That's wrong; do it this way," ask, "What were the options you considered and what motivated you to make the recommendation you did?" Or in lieu of saying, "Your recommendation doesn't comport with our strategy," ask, "How will your recommendation drive our strategic success?"

Second, if your comments contain nothing of real value, don't add them. And even before making a comment, look inside and ask, "Does what I intend to say contribute to fulfilling my conditions of satisfaction, the success and development of the other person/ people, our customers' satisfaction, and shareholder value?"

THE LIE: "I'm in charge, the grand poobah, the main muckety muck, the great and powerful Oz. I can do whatever I want to! I've earned that right."

THE TRUTH: Exercising your prerogatives has nothing to do with creating organizational success. Over time, if you depend on the job title on your business card to motivate people to do what you want them to, you're like the Wizard of Oz, invisible behind the curtain! If, however, you believe that enthusiastic contribution paves a smoother road to success than indentured servitude, you'll take another route.

THE LIE: "I know what people are thinking. I'm an 'open' guy. My people know that they can come to me with any concern, issue, or problem, and that they'll get an open hearing."

THE TRUTH: You *don't* know what others think, nor can you presume they know what you think. That's why you must create and exploit formal feedback mechanisms to get a valid sense of what people think on a continuing basis. And doing associate surveys just isn't adequate! Survey answers don't convey emotion; they don't allow for probing; they don't let you "peel the onion" to get an explicit sense of deep truth.

One CEO client who runs a Fortune 100 company spends about 10 hours a month talking with people at all levels of his company. At first, it made them feel uncomfortable, but now, they're really into it. What has he learned along the way? First, that nothing beats nose-to-nose contact. Second, when you create a high level of openness, you inherit a responsibility for what you do (and even more importantly, *don't* do) with what you learn from talking with people. You have to listen, but you can't overreact.

THE LIE: "People already understand my motives and will forgive my idiosyncratic behavior."

THE TRUTH: No, they don't understand, and no, they won't forgive you. It's funny, but as early as age five, people have a sense of how other people's behavior affects them, yet they never fully develop an appreciation for the effect their own behavior has on others. Assumptions abound.

Do you remember being in elementary school and seeing one of your teachers in the grocery store? You sheepishly said, "Hi, Mr. Smith" but you likely thought, "What's Mr. Smith doing here in the grocery store?" Despite his lofty position as your teacher, why should Mr. Smith be above going grocery shopping? A young mind doesn't know that!

When you hold a position of authority, you assume characteristics and attributes in people's minds by virtue of your position. Whether or not you think that ought to be true misses the point. If you're The Boss (pardon me, Mr. Springsteen), you're expected to conduct yourself with a level of virtue that exceeds that of mere mortals.

Heads of companies don't lay exclusive claim to the issues noted, but they're extraordinarily susceptible to them. If you are a CEO or aspire to become one, be mindful of these lies and set up processes to overturn them.

Do not ever *whittle down your aspirations to artificially bolster your performance. Instead, raise your game to bring you closer to your aspirations. That will move you* away *from fear and* toward *the best possible version of yourself!*

Governing Beliefs: Leadership from the Inside Out

To live life with meaning, it's important to realize this: The dissonance and discomfort you feel when your espoused beliefs and values collide with your actions are warnings. This pertains to your business life as well as your life in general. So every once in a while, put pen to paper (or fingers to keyboard) and write down both your beliefs and values in a granular way. Periodically, go back and add, subtract, and clarify these beliefs and values as your life gives you feedback.

Do the "lousy feeling in the pit of your stomach" test. That means when you feel really bad—I mean *really* bad due to an action you've taken or a result you've gotten in your life—reflect on this question: "Which of the beliefs or values I espouse am I violating?" Your answer to that question helps you clarify, reaffirm, or refine your perspective and act better the next time.

In that vein, never lower your expectations to accommodate your human frailty, or concoct excuses, or rationalize failure. Do not *ever* whittle down your aspirations to artificially bolster your performance. Instead, raise your game to bring you closer to your aspirations. That will move you *away* from fear and *toward* the best possible version of yourself!

My Governing Beliefs

I want to share my own governing beliefs and values as an example. I have explicit beliefs detailing what I want to stand for. Okay, I fall short from living them fully, but that's not the point. It's this: Not many things in life really matter, and the few that *do* have importance matter completely. Here goes:

1. **I believe in showing up and standing up for something I can be proud of.** Most people lament the wrongs they perceive the world has done to them, or bewail how things should be a certain way and aren't. They don't dedicate themselves to "showing up" in a way they can be proud of—being measured by their actions and being an example to others. This perspective isn't popular or sexy because it explains the world in terms of *what we owe it* rather than *what it owes us*. It rejects victim hood in favor of personal ownership.
2. **I believe in the virtues of integrity, loyalty, honesty, courage and valor, accountability for my actions, discipline, and perseverance.** I confess I have failed miserably, many times, in each of those arenas. The last two items have always been over-sized challenges for me because I grew up in a home in which family members didn't demonstrate those characteristics abundantly, so I had to find other role models. Truthfully, the virtues I embrace are all aspirations because I don't measure up to my own expectations on any of them. When I'm tested, however, I use those character traits as checkpoints. In so doing, I often make decisions that don't feel right at the time; doing what's right doesn't always feel comfortable. I usually

look back later and decide that I made a good call—again, not always, but usually.

3. **I believe in associating with those who relentlessly help me search for truth**. Most people fill their lives with others who feel sorry for them, who over sympathize with them, who validate them, who pat them on the head and say, "There, there now, you did the best you could. The problem isn't you; it's the world." They then go about making the same dumb decisions and taking the same ineffective actions over and over and over again. They develop no wisdom and stay stuck—no better off than the guys 5,000 years ago who dragged their knuckles on the ground and wrote cryptic symbols on the walls of caves. Many of us—and I've been guilty too—select friends, business associates, spouses, or significant others who give only cowardly feedback. Instead, I want people in my life who challenge me to be my best rather than fuel my shortcomings. In the midst of a problem or aftermath of a disturbing event, I want them to ask (if I don't ask myself), "What lesson is life trying to teach right now?" That said, often the quick obvious answer isn't the *real* answer, so I dig deeper . . . or wait. Sometimes, the lesson takes years to percolate and surface—often too late to readdress the initial issue itself. (Funny how the clock that life uses to cultivate my wisdom has never synchronized with my patience.) I believe that real friends—true friends, courageous friends—put truth-telling above peacekeeping. Most important, they put the welfare of their friends above the survival of comfortable friendships.

4. **I believe in pursuing the truth even if it takes me to uncomfortable places.** I frequently find that my truth represents reality *as I want it to be* rather than *reality as it is*, and I have to adjust my truth to accommodate the truth. I hate it when that happens! Yet it pays off. In a reference letter to

a peer, one of my CEO clients wrote, "When Rand opens his mouth, what comes out is the truth." That's exactly what I'm striving for.

5. **I believe that personal growth is our primary, lifelong mission.** It gets easy, especially in later years, to become imprisoned by attitudes, preconceptions, and resentments that have long outlived their usefulness. We can stay vigorous, curious, and changeable as long as we live, although these require increased rigor and tenacity as we get older. My 50s have given me my most substantial and painful growth years. John W. Gardner said, "Life is the art of drawing without an eraser." We can't change what we have done, but we can change ourselves to do it better the next time. Occasionally—not often, but occasionally—when we're really lucky, we get a "do over." That's God giving us a second chance, and we shouldn't blow it.

6. **I believe that feelings evolve out of the unique way we process our experiences.** As such, two people can develop divergent emotions from exactly the same experience, so labeling feelings (our own or other people's) as either appropriate or inappropriate makes no sense. Feelings don't come with rights and rulebooks; they just *are*. Understanding the implications of that and manifesting it in daily interactions is tough but necessary.

7. **I believe there is no wisdom without reflection and judgment.** Wisdom is imparted by experience, but not always. A huge difference lies between having ten years of experience and one year of experience ten times. For experience to result in wisdom, reflection, judgment, and behavioral adjustments have to ensue. In recent years, judgment has been given a bad rap. We're constantly admonished not to be judgmental,

yet the highest-performing among us are constantly judging. When we decide to accept a job opportunity, we're judging. When we select our friends, we're judging. When we forgive someone who has harmed us, we're judging. When judgment results in persecution, when it comes from a place of smug certainty, when it fuels our own moral superiority, it's destructive. But when it propels our productive evolution, when it promotes personal growth, when it enables sound decision-making, it's beneficial.

8. **I believe that character is both forged and revealed by the commitments we make and keep.** I'm not talking about goal setting, achievement, or purpose, although those are important components of commitment. I'm talking about keeping my word *without exception.* A promise made is considered a sacred trust regardless of the size or type. A commitment means when we say we'll do something, we actually do it and when we say we'll be somewhere, we'll show up every time!

9. **I believe that one of life's challenges—maybe the biggest—is figuring out which bridges to cross and which ones to burn.** How do we make this choice without damaging ourselves and others in an effort to achieve happiness? Historically, I've erroneously regarded honor and happiness as mutually exclusive. I've perceived honor as "doing the right thing" and happiness as "doing the selfish thing." In that vein, I frequently felt morally superior for choosing one path and overly guilty for selecting the other. In that extreme, neither is a winning choice! Accordingly, I've been a slow learner with unnecessarily rigid boundaries. Conversely, when I absolutely have to choose between those two options, I find that choosing honor over happiness is more ennobling, even if it's viscerally less pleasing.

10. **I believe that a life of purpose requires the creation of meaning.** I'm speaking practically, not idealistically here. As John W. Gardner once said, "In my experience, it's a rare person who can go through life like a stray cat, living from day to day, taking its pleasures where it can, and then dying unnoticed." In my life, I want the whole to be greater than the sum of the parts. I want it to build to a resounding crescendo I can be proud of. And at the end, I want to die in my sleep in the arms of those I love most, knowing I succeeded in balancing what I took from life with what I gave to it.

I've usually been a person who others can count on—the guy on the white horse saving the day—the "go-to guy." At the end of the game, I want the ball and I fight to take the final, decisive shot. I relish that!

I'm grateful that I'm better at walking my talk today than I was a decade or two or three ago. Still a work in progress, I do find that as I get older, my character and reputation are increasingly what I cherish most and that without exception, they are more easily protected and defended than they are recovered, once lost.

This summarizes my core governing beliefs, and I know I'd get much higher grades in elocution than execution.

Now it's your turn. What do you believe, where do you stand, and what are you doing to live your beliefs and values?

Keeping promises is a function of integrity and good manners, no excuses allowed. I promise you that paying attention to all *of your commitments will make you much more effective, so my question is this: "Do you want to follow the example* of *others or be the example* for *others?"*

Your Commitments Count

Whether you're an executive or aspire to be, if you dedicate yourself to keeping all of your commitments, you'll increase your likelihood of success. If you're thinking "my follow-through is stellar," review the following examples and then reconsider that position:

- Brad was invited to attend a dinner on November 1st. He received the invitation and responded in the affirmative on October 1st. On the day of the dinner, Brad didn't really feel like going, so he called and begged off.
- As a sales executive, Allison had to commit annually to achieving a revenue figure for the following year. In October of one year, she committed to producing $10 million in the next. By the following June, Allison knew there was no way she could hit her number, so she began giving excuses to her boss. "The competition's pricing was too aggressive; our product line isn't diverse enough." Yada, yada, yada.
- My voice mail message had this greeting: "Hi, this is Rand. I can't take your call right now, but if it's before noon I'll get back to you by the close of business today. If it's afternoon,

I'll return your call no later than noon tomorrow." After about a month, a couple of my clients reminded me that I hadn't, in fact, returned their calls as guaranteed in my message. My initial reaction was "so what's the big deal? I got back to them each within a day." Then one of them reminded me I have no right to vigorously insist that she keep her commitments if I don't. She was right. I changed my message.

Excuses, Excuses

Few people make a habit of keeping every commitment they make. Frequently, they say they'll do something or be somewhere when they really mean that they will if it suits them or unless a better opportunity shows up. Much of the time, commitments get quietly dismissed with excuses like these:

- "They won't care if I don't show up. Plenty of other people will be there. I won't be missed."
- "C'mon! Nobody's perfect! Besides, it's not that big of a deal."
- "So what if I was late for the appointment. Nobody got mad and other people were late also."
- "I know I told Sarah I'd have her performance appraisal done by today. Other stuff came up; she'll have to understand."

Keeping promises is a function of integrity and good manners, no excuses allowed. I promise you that paying attention to *all* of your commitments will make you much more effective, so my question is this: "Do you want to follow the example *of* others or be the example *for* others?"

Decide to Follow Through No Matter What

Beginning right now, decide to make a priority of keeping all of your commitments, every one. *Don't make 'em if you're not sure you can keep 'em.*

That means don't tell your daughter you'll be at her soccer game when you really mean *if* work doesn't interfere. Live by the following credo: "Beginning today, I will do what I say I will do, the way I say (or imply) I will do it, when I say I will do it—every time."

Those times when you fail to keep your promise (and you will), don't let yourself off the hook. Discern the real reason for your transgression and make appropriate adjustments to your commitments, your follow-through, or both.

When you do, the rewards you accrue will be significant!

The overall responsibility of the CEO is to define, create, and distribute "value" for all of the company's stakeholders, over time.

Jump on Your CEO's Bandwagon

A year ago, one of my CEO clients asked me to create a brief job description for him to use for an all-associate presentation. He added his own meat to my bones and used the presentation to provoke an ongoing, company-wide dialogue about the role of the CEO—and what people can do to augment their contribution to the company. Here's a brief summary of that job description:

The overall responsibility of the **CEO is to define, create, and distribute "value" for all of the company's stakeholders, over time**. Each stakeholder group defines and prioritizes the elements of value differently. The CEO must fulfill these priorities without compromising away the interest of any stakeholder group in the process.

The CEO's three primary jobs are:

- strategy formulation,
- organizational transformation, and
- strategy execution.

These three accountabilities have to be accomplished against a backdrop of major organizational challenges. The most prevalent of these challenges are:

- building a strong customer base,
- securing and maintaining support from capital markets, and
- *establishing "leadership" and an effective top-management team.*

If you are a CEO, this definition requires you to help associates (1) understand how to do their jobs in a way that will make you successful in doing yours and (2) internalize why they should care about that.

If you are not a CEO, you still have a big stake in the growth and success of your company. To that end, take these 11 actions to support your CEO's success:

1. Start a discussion group to dig deeper into these concepts and what you can do, in your own world, to drive success along these dimensions.
2. Distinguish relevant procedures and processes from waste, then eliminate the waste.
3. Make yourself more valuable every day. Read business books; volunteer for task forces that expand your horizons; become disciplined in applying what you learn. (Remember, knowledge is not power; the relevant application of knowledge is power!)
4. Be a leader as well as a manager. "Manager" is a job; "leader" is a reputation. If you believe that gaining people's commitment is more important than getting their obedience, your actions must reflect that.

5. Support your organization with your actions and words. NEVER . . . EVER . . . EVER fall into the trap of being the company naysayer.
6. Never speculate out loud. (Remember, the degree to which people ascribe factual accuracy to everything you say is directly proportional to the size of your paycheck.)
7. Protect your company's customers. Resist "throttling back" on customer service, even during a recession. View a lousy economy as an opportunity to ramp up customer focus and skewer competitors.
8. Communicate obsessively. Remember that listening is a more important skill than talking, and that listening to understand is more important than simply listening to respond.
9. Engage in productive risk-taking. Never lapse into risk-averse behavior.
10. Make your priorities and "marching orders" crystal clear. During uncertain times, people need a degree of certainty, so give them information they can count on.
11. Challenge your own thinking, and that of others, with probing questions that will keep attention focused on what matters. (See the side bar for a powerful example of this.)

Use these ideas to get on track toward tough-minded leadership!

Sometimes It Just Takes One Question

Fifteen years ago, I had about 1,200 people in more than a dozen different functions reporting to me. From among that group, a cross-functional team was in the process of developing a new product. As the project's sponsor, I operated at arm's length, giving the leader latitude to make decisions and direct activities.

During a team meeting, a "food fight" broke out about priorities among the marketing people, actuaries, and information technology staff involved. From what I heard (I wasn't present), it got nasty and personal—lots of name-calling and finger-pointing. During a cooling-off break, the team leader found me and asked me to help team members get back on track. Still, the "fight" continued. I simply observed for about five minutes, then gave the "time-out" signal and inquired if I could ask the group a question.

With their okay, I asked the following question in a highly measured tone: "What does any of this behavior have to do with creating value for our customers?"

Silence.

Then I got up and left.

To a person, the team members thanked me later for getting their meeting back on track. Sometimes it just takes one question.

Being open is a precondition for objectivity. The filters that edit out information for most people don't exist for the most successful executives. For these few, ego boundaries can be extremely permeable; they don't require validation.

Objectivity: An Executive's Most Undervalued Attribute

I work with executive officers of both large and small corporations, all with varied experiences and backgrounds. Some are marketers; others are financial people. Some come from human resources; others from sales.

Invariably every one of them asks the same question at some point in our relationship. It's this: "Rand, is there any single attribute that you believe is a precondition for success as a senior executive?" I pause unnecessarily as if to ponder all of the implications of the question, but I have only one answer. It's this: Objectivity.

First, a bit of groundwork. I spend a lot of time convincing people that the world exists in shades of gray. That includes the disciplines of analysis and decision-making where there's a lot of room between absolute subjectivity and absolute objectivity. Here's the problem: *Most people, in most situations, convince themselves that they are being objective when they're not!*

Typically, people develop a worldview based on their life experiences. Along the road, they subconsciously conclude that their worldview represents reality—*objective* reality. As they process information, they edit out what doesn't conform to their preconceptions. They also aggressively seek out and consume information that affirms their perspectives.

Effective executives simply don't do that!

Given that, exactly what does objectivity look like?

Peter Senge, author of *The Fifth Discipline*, has referred to the concept of openness, which takes two forms: reflective and participative. "Reflective" refers to the ability to question one's own preconceptions, subjecting them to relentless scrutiny and evaluation. It also requires an attitude that invites critical input from the outside—an ability most executives *believe* they embody, but don't.

"Participative" is the ability to share one's perspective with others in a way that encourages them to employ their own reflective openness.

Being open is a precondition for objectivity. The filters that edit out information for most people don't exist for the most successful executives. For these few, ego boundaries can be extremely permeable; they don't require validation.

In a former life as a COO, my boss once admonished me, "Remember, you used to get paid to have great answers; now you get paid to ask great questions." I didn't fully appreciate the implications of that advice at the time, but I do now.

Objectivity requires a relentless pursuit of the truth. In addition to judgment, which by definition is subjective, it must include the separation of one's ego and emotional investment from that search—a difficult habit to conquer.

While advising a Fortune 100 CEO, I regularly attended his results reviews with his executive team. He'd constantly ask questions, not to second-guess his people but to:

- adjust his thinking on issues when required
- develop a comfort level with their thinking
- learn as much as possible about the competitive dynamics of their businesses
- serve as a role model for them as they lead their businesses and functions
- identify his areas of priority

As a leader, how objective are you?

Most people spend their professional lives focused on improving their weaknesses. Whether you're an entrepreneur, an executive, or aspire to be either, you've probably told yourself (or been told by managers or corporate HR staffers) that success requires well-roundedness. Not quite!

Your Strengths Will Give You Leverage; Your Weaknesses Never Will

As baseball's last .400 hitter in 1941, Ted Williams's exceptional path of success was laid in his youth. While Ted was still very young, people noticed his sharp perception of time/space relationships, his quick reflexes, and his incredible hand-eye coordination.

When he began to play baseball as a young boy, these talents served him well. He enjoyed rapid success and worked diligently to hone his hitting skills. As he became more successful, his love of the game developed. Increasingly, he pushed himself harder to improve, but it wasn't hard or tedious work for Ted. While baseball required tremendous effort, to him it seemed effortless because he loved what he was doing.

In both World War II and the Korean War, Ted served his country as a pilot, or maybe I should say *the* pilot. Those who served with him called him one of the greatest military pilots ever.

The same talents, attributes, skills, and knowledge that propelled his baseball success made him a strong combat aviator.

And there's more. During and after his baseball career, Ted's love of fly-fishing developed and grew. He became an award winner. Again, his hand-eye coordination, highly developed sense of time and space, love of the sport, and diligent practice fueled his success.

Now that you've read the "what," here's the "so what."

Most people spend their professional lives focused on improving their weaknesses. Whether you're an entrepreneur, an executive, or aspire to be either, you've probably told yourself that success requires well-roundedness. If your strength is "x," you also have to become adept at "y" to succeed.

Not quite!

Peter Drucker had it right when he said that a manager's primary job is to make strength productive and render weakness irrelevant, that the most effective competitive strategies rely first on strength. Many of today's executives are convinced, however, that while strengths should be engaged and deployed, weaknesses should be the focus of their people development initiatives.

Here's the tough-minded truth: Most weaknesses improve slightly with *lots* of work, money, and time, but they're still weaknesses. What's the real requirement for personal success? It's strength, and the equation looks like this:

STRENGTH = talents *x* attributes *x* knowledge *x* skills *x* passion

Here are my definitions of the components:

Talents are genetic strengths. They are gifts and they are immutable. Take a look at the talents noted in the Ted Williams story. They can be augmented by the other elements that contribute to strength, but if you're tone deaf, a year of training with Andrea Boccelli won't make you a world-class tenor.

Remember, everyone has specific, unique talents. Ignoring them always creates a longing later in life, so don't ignore yours.

Attributes are qualities of morality, character or personality initiated genetically and developed primarily in childhood. They include discipline, courage, emotional endurance, optimism, honesty, and persistence. A recent study found that, while these traits can develop further later in life with patience, persistence, practice, and reinforcement, they're typically 80 percent hard-wired by the age of 18. The degree and nature of parental love—the aggregate of actions parents take with their children to instill self-worth and inspire exploration in a safe and supportive environment—do more to develop specific attributes (for better or worse) than any other factor. Given that fact, this presents an enormous challenge.

Knowledge represents the level of conceptual and factual learning from the most basic (curiosity) to the most mature (perspective). In most companies, the acquisition of knowledge is deemed to be synonymous with professional development. For example, if John has a problem with collaboration, he's sent to a seminar to learn collaborative skills. When John returns, he may have learned a lot *about* collaboration, but he won't have permanently changed his behavior or improved his performance.

Skills are strengths performing specific tasks. If knowledge is about the *what*, skills are about the *how*. In business, we get paid for doing, not for knowing.

Passion develops when attributes, skills, talent, and knowledge converge. Its energy then feeds the development of even higher levels of skill and knowledge, which in turn spark additional passion. You get the idea. A quick word to the wise: To the observer, passion does not always look like a Jack Welch-type exec on steroids. For example, one of my clients was roundly criticized for lacking passion. In reality, he just didn't display his passion in an overt, fist-shaking, evangelical way. Inside, he had plenty of zest and commitment.

Whether you're concerned with your own improvement, the development of others, or both, here's the lesson: *Personal strength evolves out of a messy, non-linear collision of experiences in childhood.* Further (my apologies to Jim Collins), going from "good to great" requires the ongoing development and leverage of existing strengths as well as implementing multidimensional strategies that address the distinct elements of strength appropriately.

Look for the Passion

A number of years ago, I led a strategy consulting session for a large consulting firm. Part of my challenge was helping corporate executives think strategically. Strategic thinking and strategic planning are distinct but equally important disciplines. As a practical matter, strategic plans are frequently and inappropriately linear extrapolations of the past while strategic thinking requires vision and creativity, or something called "what if" thinking.

In those days, I invariably took clients through a SWOT (strengths, weaknesses, opportunities, and threats) analysis. Have you done these? Executives detail their organization's current strengths and weaknesses as well as current and prospective competitive, economic, and regulatory opportunities and threats. The ultimate objective is to develop plans that enable an organization to leverage the strengths (S) and improve the weaknesses (W) while exploiting the opportunities (O) and alleviating the threats (T).

During these sessions, executives almost always focused on weaknesses, thinking, "Why should we spend our time doing anything about our strengths? They're already strengths!"

Yet leveraging existing strengths is almost always less expensive and time-consuming than building or recruiting new ones. With individuals, the challenge is similar. People almost always want to focus on improving their weaknesses. I constantly hear comments like this: "My company's CEO thinks I'm a really great creative thinker but my 'follow-through' isn't as good as it needs to be."

This calls for crafting a development plan focused on improving follow-through, right? But here's the problem: Depending on how large the deficit, this person's follow-through skills could become marginally better through training and development, and only after putting in a lot of work. Both the manager and the individual might be better off figuring out ways to leverage his *strengths* for the good of the organization.

Now, I'm not advocating the neglect of deficiencies. But I do believe leaders expend too much energy and money on deficiencies and not enough to augment and deploy capabilities. They often neglect this equally important consideration: What is the person *really* passionate about?

Remember this when taking on a new job:
You have six months maximum to establish and cement your leadership agenda. *That includes establishing your expectations for performance and then evaluating and selecting key people. Do your assessments and make your big decisions quickly, especially regarding people.*

Leaders, You Have 6 Months to Cement Your Agenda

Ken had just become president of a medium-sized pharmaceutical company. He had been my client when he led a $2 billion division of a similar but much larger company. At his new position for about a month, he wanted to share his observations and solicit my feedback on his plans over lunch. I arrived at the appointed time, giddy and eager to help him create a wildly successful enterprise.

Ken walked me through the challenges that he faced, the competitive advantages his company enjoyed, the ways he intended to exploit those as well as deal with current and prospective obstacles that could derail them. We discussed his competitors, "wedge issues," internal processes, and, finally, the quality of his leadership team.

That last subject extended our lunch meeting through dinner.

Ken told me about his 10 direct reports. Nine of them were rock-solid players, impressive high flyers. But the struggling team member was Brett, the head of Sales. Despite high-quality marketing, an enviable product portfolio, and a consistently replenished pipeline, the company's sales performance was anemic. Ken knew that if he left this situation to linger, it could kill the company. Lest you think our first thought was "sales aren't great so let's blame the sales guy," it wasn't. I walked Ken through the complex web of issues that were likely driving sales results. It really was the sales guy.

Now, Ken and I have always been great partners in getting to the right answers for the right reasons. Ken loved the "thrust and parry" of an aggressive, one-on-one exchange, while I always love working with people who relish having their preconceptions challenged. I truly enjoy being the instigator of changed perspectives.

With his background in sales and marketing, Ken had expertise in all aspects of buyer conversion, plus he honed his skills in leadership development and coaching over his 20-year career. Ken had one fatal flaw: *He believed that with enough personal exposure to himself, ANYONE could become great*, including Brent. So during our lengthy discussion, Ken pitched the idea that "Brent could be saved." I wasn't buying it.

I am prone to speak bluntly, but I use blunt talk sparingly so I don't diminish its impact. In this case, the future of the company depended on its CEO, Ken, seeing this personnel challenge objectively. Varnishing the truth with "weasel words" would not have worked.

Migrating from coach to consultant, consigliore, and admonisher-in-chief, I listened to his well-crafted argument first and then launched this speech: "Listen carefully, Ken. What I'm about to tell you could save you! I think we're at a point at which hubris is affecting your thinking."

I had his attention and conveyed these points:

- You're new in this position; you don't have time to invest in folly.
- Brent is performing unacceptably. You believe he can get better if you spend a considerable amount of time coaching him.
- You have no real evidence that his issues are susceptible to a coaching or mentoring solution.
- This is not a high-leverage way for you to spend your time—especially since you know 25 other people who could do a far superior job in sales.
- If Brent fails, you fail. Even if he improves, it'll take a long time.

These points may apply to your situation, too. Remember this when taking on a new job: *You have six months maximum to establish and cement your leadership agenda.* That includes conveying your expectations for performance and then evaluating and selecting key people. Do your assessments and make your big decisions quickly, especially regarding people.

If you've been as successful as Ken, you'll likely assume you can fix any problem with the force of your will. You cannot.

As humans, we tend to cling to our own perspectives as if they represent the *truth rather than merely* our *truth. It's a protective mechanism that helps make sense out of nonsense, brings order to chaos, and validates personal rules for how the world works.*

The Tough-Minded Truth: Get Real, Get Tough, Get Going

I was shopping for a new tennis racquet in a store in northern Montgomery County, Maryland. The store had recently changed hands after the previous owner declared bankruptcy. The new proprietor greeted me with a hearty "good morning." I asked about the details of the transfer of ownership and learned that he'd acquired the furniture, fixtures, and stock from the previous owner for a reasonable price. He'd also assumed the rental commitment.

After I told him what I did for a living, I asked, "Given the failure of the prior ownership to make a go of the business, what are you doing to improve the odds that your result will be different?" His look of fear, anger, and confusion plus his response—"that's really none of your business"—told me he'd never considered the question.

Most businesses don't survive to see their 10th anniversary. The reasons cited in business publications are valid but insufficient, including:

- inadequate capital
- lack of management controls
- entrepreneurs/CEOs/business owners who are proficient in their technical specialty, but who don't have the requisite skills to lead and manage a business
- insignificant or nonexistent differentiation
- strategic plans that wind up as credenza ornaments.

These "reasons" are actually symptoms of this bigger problem: *Most business owners do an inadequate job of driving toward what I call the tough-minded truth.*

What is the Tough-Minded Truth?

Webster defines "truth" as "the body of real things, events, and facts." The operative words are "real" and "facts." Real facts are unassailable; they're indisputable; they just *are*. They pass the test of "reasonable scientific certainty."

For example, 2 + 2 = 4 is a fact, but the statement "our company went out of business because of a recession" is not a fact.

The tough-minded truth is a state of certainty to which business people must aspire. It implies fact-based analysis and decision-making. It differentiates facts from legitimate but incomplete intuition. It requires the egoless testing of assumptions and the relentless scrutiny of preconceptions. It explains results in terms of valid reasons but never translates reasons into excuses.

Arriving at the tough-minded truth is difficult. As humans, we tend to cling to our own perspectives as if they represent *the* truth rather than merely *our* truth. It's a protective mechanism that helps make sense out of nonsense, brings order to chaos, and validates personal rules for how the world works.

The problem is, clinging to such a narrow view of truth disables organizational and personal success and growth.

Successful people drive to adopt the tough-minded truth for these two reasons:

1. **Tough-minded truth infuses any situation with reality—a precondition for success.** Business decisions must be made and actions taken based on a foundation of reality, not hoped-for or half-true reality. Without it, organizations become ineffective and eventually wither and die. Most executives accept this, but only as an abstract idea. When it comes to specific issues, they fall short. Why? The truth often hurts and makes us resist feeling bad in the short-term, even if there's a long-term payback for doing so.
2. **Tough-minded truth develops wisdom.** Wisdom enables your tomorrow to look different than your yesterday. No one gets through life without getting his or her backside kicked. While it's important to "pick yourself up, dust yourself off, and start all over again," that recommendation is incomplete because, as the saying goes, "some people have 10 years of experience; others have one year, 10 times."

Dealing with reality is a primary, maybe *the* primary, challenge you face as a business leader. Without it, you'll never achieve your dreams. With it, almost anything is possible.

To Become Tough-minded, You Must
Get Real, Get Tough,* and *Get Going

Get Real.

This step is about rigorous, relentless honesty and objectivity. It means confronting situations *as they are,* not as you'd like them to be.

Get Tough.

This step deals with developing the thick skin and character required to be tough-minded as a way of life but does not imply hard-headedness or cold-heartedness. The former (hard-headedness) characterizes people who resist input or feedback that challenges their preconceptions; the latter (cold-heartedness) describes those who punish either themselves or others for the way things are.

Get Going.

Many people are adept at honesty, objectivity, and tough-mindedness but unfortunately accomplish nothing. They know what to do, but they never actually do it. Remember this: *Life rewards action.*

I'm not recommending that you adopt a "time management system" wholesale. You wouldn't do it, anyway. Rather, grab the "low-hanging fruit" first to build momentum. It will set you up to succeed.

Why Start with the End in Mind

My client John had been operating a pair of successful auto dealerships. Although his personal income approached a million dollars a year, he was on the treadmill of financial success but personal oblivion. This one symptom tells an ugly story: He hadn't taken a family vacation in five years.

Today, he owns five auto dealerships, his net worth tripled in three years, and his personal income has doubled. But here's the best result: Last year, John worked only 150 days! That means he took off 215 days—yes, 215 *full* days away from phone calls, emails, and work, period! What turned this ugly story into a beautiful one? John stopped buying into the notion that financial success required him to become a martyr for his business.

That desire led him to implement processes that made him personally more effective at work. I call it *effective* rather than *productive* for a reason. "Productive" implies doing more in less time; personal effectiveness isn't about that. As Stephen Covey would say, it's about starting with the end in mind. In John's case, he started by analyzing the kind of life he wanted, then put new systems in place to achieve that.

I'm not recommending that you adopt a "time management system" wholesale. You wouldn't do it, anyway. I do recommend adopting one or more of the following recommendations. Grab the "low-hanging fruit" first to build momentum. It will set you up to succeed.

1. **Focus your energy on your life's priorities.**

   Among the hundreds of executives I've worked with on personal effectiveness, the successful ones start by identifying their priorities in the following areas: financial, professional, physical, spiritual, emotional, intellectual, familial, and social. From there, they plan their calendars and activities around their objectives in all of these areas.

   If you're saying, "easier said than done," you're right. Yet worthwhile doesn't mean easy. If you don't believe you can follow this recommendation, then you're right again. You can only do what you *believe* you can do.

2. **Know your strengths and passions, and spend your time hooking into them.**

   Spending time attempting to master skills you hate doing completely wastes your time. Eight years ago, a friend started a business that exceeded $12 million in annual revenue. She used to go crazy trying to master all of the elements of her business. Two years ago, she had an epiphany and changed her approach. Today, she spends her time developing and marketing new products for her business—activities that reflect her strengths and true passion. She's learned to delegate other business and personal activities, including paying her personal bills. By completely aligning her life around her strengths and passions, she's happier and much more effective in everything she does.

3. **Delegate, but don't abdicate.**

   Many successful business leaders erroneously believe that *delegation* means *abdication*. Here's my rule of thumb: Before you assign work, develop confidence in the competence of the individual or team to whom you're delegating. Understand that competence is task-specific and situation-specific. Remember, fixing problems created by poorly delegating takes lots of time and money.

4. **Conduct meetings that mean more than eating donuts.**

   Because attending meetings is the biggest time trap for most business leaders, it's tempting to conduct no meetings at all. Before you do that, consider the following three factors. First, acknowledge that some decisions and solutions require airing out differing perspectives. Second, getting a consistent message out is better served by communicating it *one time* to an entire team instead of multiple times to disparate parties. Third, building consensus and buy-in usually requires dialogue among members of a team.

   What's a better solution? Learning to run meetings well using proven management and problem-solving tools. Effective meeting management requires the use of agendas, minutes, charters, and ground rules; problem-solving tools include cause and effect diagrams, Pareto charts, force field analysis, nominal group technique, and more. When meetings are planned and executed well, you'll produce the results and stimulate the relevant action you want.

5. **Make technology your servant, not the other way around.**

   Technology should facilitate effectiveness, not create servitude. So if you've conditioned people to expect you to be available 24/7, your priorities will blend into a mush of "just more stuff." It's insane to believe that being totally connected 100% of the time is required to do business, although frequently, it helps insecure people who create little or no real value feel relevant. I know you know what I mean.

6. **At the end of the day, put your stuff away.**

   It's just like you learned in kindergarten. Put everything where it belongs at the end of your work day, including both your hard mail and email. Do not leave them lurking in your in-baskets (real or virtual). Do them, delegate them, defer them, or ditch them. For more on this subject, read *Getting Things Done* by David Allen.

7. **Initiate and maintain a pattern of self-care.**

   If you feel you're taking care of everyone else in your life but yourself, start focusing more on you. Diet, exercise, meditation, or simply pausing to reflect can develop your capacity to live "in the moment" in a healthy way. When you take this to heart, your work life and your personal life become more rewarding.

8. **Keep the commitments you make.**

   Suffice it to say that you'll be more effective if you carefully weigh the commitments you take on, and then religiously keep those you selected.

Whether you're creating a business plan or criteria for a performance evaluation, I suggest you have well-written goals that meet five acid tests, symbolized by the acronym S•M•A•R•T.

Make Sure You Set S•M•A•R•T Goals

Your ability to manage your business, your work, your budget, your people, and yourself depends on differentiating well-crafted business goals from poorly conceived ones. The following are stated performance goals from two clients of mine:

- Ensure that the business makes good investment decisions.
- Deliver financial results for year end while maintaining a high quality of execution.

I ask you, what do these goals have in common? Answer: Neither is a legitimate goal or objective. Yes, both of these statements provide *categories* for objectives, but neither meets the criteria for a well-written business *goal*.

Whether you're creating a business plan or criteria for a performance evaluation, I suggest you have well-written goals that meet five acid tests, symbolized by the acronym S•M•A•R•T. Make sure they are:

- ***Specific.*** The goal "work out with a personal trainer three times a week" is much more specific than "start exercising." Both of the goals cited earlier were too general to be workable.
- ***Measurable.*** If you can't measure it, you can't manage it. But that doesn't mean the measures have to be in dollars. If your goal is not measurable, however, it's either an aspiration, a good idea, or a hallucination. (I used to work for a guy who, when reviewing generic, immeasurable goals would ask, "So, how do I know when we can declare victory?")
- ***Attainable.*** When you define desired goals, you learn a lot about goal setting and about yourself. Goals that initially seem like they "stretch" you too much become perfectly reasonable before very long. Remember, though, "attainable" doesn't mean easy. In 1970, martial artist Bruce Lee wrote the following: "By 1980, I will be the best known Oriental movie star in the United States and I will have secured $10 million." Now there's a goal—and one he met. Stretch goals engender commitment, activate energetic responses, stimulate creative action steps, and close the exit doors on excuses. Make sure that "attainable" becomes more challenging for you over time.
- ***Realistic.*** This is the first cousin of "attainable." If you're 65 years old without a college education, it's unreasonable to set a goal to "become a world-class neurosurgeon within five years." Perhaps it's not unreasonable to aspire to "obtain a college degree and then a medical degree within 10 years" if you are totally committed to doing so. (Personally, I gave up the dream of being Mick Jagger about 25 years ago!)
- ***Time-bound.*** By when do you intend to achieve your goal? If you're a sales person, a plan to "produce $10 million in new business by year end" has teeth. Without including your target date, though, your goal has no teeth.

Although goal setting is more an art than a science, I can unequivocally say that virtually all high achievers are goal setters. Why? Because setting goals helps them become who they want to be; achieving goals helps them determine who they want to become after that!

And that's true for you, too.

Take These Points to Heart to Help You Embrace Your Goals

- Goals are commitments. Viewing them that way will ensure greater diligence. If it doesn't, ask this question: "How am I dealing with other commitments in my life?"
- Goals should represent aspirations that you can control or significantly influence. Otherwise, they'll become a source of frustration and you'll likely abandon them.
- Goals you set require action plans. That means "chunking down" your goal into interim measures and incremental steps to get there. These must specify the "who," the "when," the "what" (resources necessary), and the feedback mechanisms you'll use to track progress.

Consider These Obstacles You Must Overcome

- It's not your plan that achieves results; *you* do. Don't let your plans gather dust like they're credenza ornaments.
- Personal change is difficult. Here's something most goal-setting literature doesn't tell you: *If you aren't comfortable setting goals, doing so can be a really scary proposition.* Remember, when you create goals and plans, your actions will take place sometime in the future, so your enthusiasm for doing what you plan to do will diminish when you confront the difficulty of doing it. Making a commitment seems easy when its implications are remote and abstract; it's another matter when that commitment is imminent and concrete. Therefore, to achieve your goals, *your resolve has to be greater than your resistance.*
- Without accountability, goal setting wastes your time. If your goals remain your personal secret, you're only accountable to yourself; that's insufficient. Share your goals and review your progress with someone invested in your success.

Organizations that rely on formal rules to impose restrictions and govern behavior typically have a tough time attracting and retaining a creative, enthusiastic workforce. I've seen lots of companies populated by drones; it's not a pretty sight.

Punishing the Many to Control the Few

I disdain bureaucracy. However, that doesn't mean I disdain procedures.

My definition of bureaucracy is "policies and/or procedures that create no value for stakeholders." So, for example, I don't consider procedures governing the conduct and frequency of performance reviews to be bureaucracy. But if they're installed and no one uses them, that's another story.

Here's a personal anecdote: In a previous work life, a group of senior leaders in a large organization reported to me. At a staff meeting one Friday, one of these people brought up "casual Fridays," which we had implemented about a year before. He cited a couple of examples of people who were regularly abusing our Friday dress code and then proposed we eliminate casual days because of these violations. When I flatly refused, he looked perplexed and asked, "How are we going to eliminate this problem if we allow people to abuse the system?" I inquired how many people were creating this problem, while wondering why I was spending my time on this issue. A quick tally revealed that less than five percent of the associate population was going too far with the concept of "casual Fridays."

"I have an idea," I said. "Why don't all of you manage your own individual problems?" The management team met this suggestion with blank expressions, so I continued, "If you have one or two people in need of clarification, talk to them. Does it make sense to punish the others who enjoy casual days and whose attire remains appropriate for a business environment?"

We agreed to deal with the exceptions. But it raised this question: How many managers do not appropriately conduct one-on-one discussions to deal with issues, instead depending on general pronouncements, remote edicts, or impersonal policies, processes, and procedures?

Organizations that rely on formal rules to impose restrictions and govern behavior typically have a tough time attracting and retaining a creative, enthusiastic workforce. I've seen lots of companies populated by drones; it's not a pretty sight.

Where formal policies and procedures need to exist, organizational leaders should provide context. People have a right and a good reason to know why those rules exist and the value they create. Leaders benefit because it's in their interest to have people supporting decisions voluntarily and with enthusiasm.

Isn't it true that *self-discipline* is almost always more productive than *imposed discipline*?

Successful leaders start with the end in mind. That end is the fulfillment of the organization's mission through the achievement of planned results. They accept the notion that the right to impose their will does not automatically confer the wisdom to use it judiciously and infrequently.

How Can You Lead When They Always Agree with You?

I always ask my clients, "What do you do to stimulate disagreement in your organization?" Most of the time, the response is, "Huh?" Once in a while, a client will state with pride that she rarely encounters disagreement—that the people in her organization serve at her pleasure and almost always do her bidding without question. Infrequently, I'll encounter a leader who "gets it." In this case, "gets it" means the following.

Successful leaders recognize that great ideas and solutions emerge from all quarters and that they, themselves, haven't cornered the market on wisdom. They start with the end in mind. That end is the fulfillment of the organization's mission through the achievement of planned results. They accept the notion that the right to impose their will does not automatically confer the wisdom to use it judiciously and infrequently.

These unusually gifted leaders "walk their talk." They act to demonstrate their commitment to the tough-minded truth, regardless of its origin.

For example, successful leaders:

- always encourage and sometimes reward people for disagreement; they don't shoot the messenger.
- employ language in decision-making meetings that evokes contrary points of view.
- read body language well, and when they see people signaling disagreement, insist on their expressing it.
- hire people whose perspectives, preconceptions, ideas, and approaches to problem solving differ from their own, constructing their team with an eye for mavericks.
- constantly and consistently ratchet up expectations of themselves and others.
- model the essence of constructive conflict.
- use questions to stimulate dialogue.
- value lifelong learning and constantly seek more.

Effective executives, especially senior executives, accept the proposition that while earlier in their careers they got paid to have *good* answers, they now get paid to ask *great* questions. When someone proposes an idea to increase sales, for example, an effective executive might ask, "What do you think the implications are for our order-fulfillment commitments?" or "What were the alternatives you considered before making this recommendation?"

Asking questions is powerful. They can facilitate executive learning; they can impart a more strategic perspective; and they can reveal the quality of thinking that went into a recommendation.

All too often, questions are asked with implied judgment or a tone of indictment. When properly formulated, however, they can serve many a powerful purpose. Along with the other actions of tough-minded leaders noted above, they can encourage diversity, creativity, and a broader base for problem solving.

Are you constantly asking *great* questions?

We always, always impose subjective assessments on data when we convert it to useful information, and from there, to conclusions and decisions. If you don't acknowledge that premise and construct mechanisms to account for it, you'll be in trouble.

What Undermines Effective Decision-Making?

As part of an engagement with a client, an insurer, I walked the executive leadership team through a discussion of company strengths and weaknesses as well as external opportunities and threats. I stood at the white board posting their answers as the discussion migrated to an assessment of the independent insurance agencies that represented them.

The chief marketing officer, an enthusiastic, optimistic guy, said, "Our agents love us." When I asked if I should add that to the list of internal strengths already enumerated, he energetically replied "yes." Then, with a somewhat bewildered look on my face, I asked if anyone had any questions or comments to add to his point. Everyone in the room shook his/her head no, and we moved on to the next issue.

For the next 15 minutes or so, I kept hoping someone would request a return to "our agents love us." No one did. I became impatient, saw the opportunity to make a point, and seized it.

Looking at the CEO, I asked, "Can we return to the comment about the esteem in which your agents hold the company?" Although he said "certainly," the look on his face implied, "Certainly, but I'd rather not."

I began, "You all agreed with the point that your agents love you. Correct?"

The team members shook their heads in agreement.

"May I drill down a bit and ask you a few questions about that assertion?" I asked.

"Fine," the CEO responded tepidly.

I took a deep breath and then launched. "Do all of your agents really love you? Do you really care if all of your agents love you? If they don't all love you, which ones do? Are the ones who actually do love you, the ones making you money? What are you doing about those who don't?"

I continued with a few more questions, but you get the point.

This team had lapsed into two of the primary miscues that undermine effective team decision-making—groupthink and rushing to judgment. During our ensuing discussion, they acknowledged that facts not currently in evidence were required before asserting that "our agents love us." The next week, the team members assembled specific data that led them to a different, more quantified conclusion.

The bottom line—the "why you should give a damn" point—is, you may believe that you always make objective decisions based solely on facts, but you don't. The reason? You're human! We always, always impose subjective assessments on data when we convert it to useful information, and from there, to conclusions and decisions. If you don't acknowledge that premise and construct mechanisms to account for it, you'll be in trouble.

In Malcolm Gladwell's book *Blink,* he detailed instances when intuition either supplemented or replaced analysis in successful decisions. While I believe intuition is valuable, I recommend using it to supplement a quantified business case rather than alone or the other way around. Regardless, too many "quant-jocks" view intuition as guesswork; too many right-brainers view statistics with suspicion.

Additional Causes of Ineffective Decision Making

- **Hubris.** We're the best. We're the smartest. We're the Masters of the Universe. (But, of course, we're humble.)
- **Excessive optimism.** Optimism is good unless it turns you into a Pollyanna. I once knew a CFO I referred to as Dr. No. One time during a meeting break, Dr. No pulled me aside and asked, "You wanna know how I got so pessimistic? By financing optimists."
- **Confirmation bias.** That's when one screens out data that don't support a business case or a preconception. Anyone who's ever done a sales presentation knows all about this. However, I've seen it applied in other areas with more chilling effect. For example, I witnessed a group of scientists at a pharma discount a number that didn't support a particular conclusion. I can only speculate on how often this happens when a physician has an ego investment in a diagnosis. (Read Dr. Jerome Groopman's book *How Doctors Think* for more on this subject.)

- **Reliance on easily accessible information.** It's easier to use available data to prove a point or make a decision than to dig for the truth.
- **Assumption that our worldviews, beliefs, thinking, and emotions are facts.** It's a natural, automatic, subconscious human reaction to make this assumption. From that, we subconsciously conclude that any worldviews, beliefs, thinking, and emotions that contradict our own are, by definition, wrong.

As a business leader, it's vital that you explicitly understand how you and your team make decisions. Don't delude yourself by ascribing unjustifiable objectivity to a process that's totally human, and therefore imperfect. The frequency with which you revisit assumptions and decisions ought to be proportional to the magnitude of the risk, the probability of failure, and the balance between intuition and facts.

Unless you're a solopreneur, you can't—and it isn't wise to—make all decisions yourself. Success requires recognizing that the notion of the well-rounded executive is a myth. You need to complement your personal strengths with people who have strengths you don't.

Making the Right Decisions Right

Whether you lead your own firm or someone else's, you're required to make the right decisions, and then to make them right. Here's a brief overview of what this takes.

First, what are the right decisions?

Unless you're a solopreneur, you can't—and it isn't wise to—make all decisions yourself. Success requires recognizing that the notion of the well-rounded executive is a myth. You need to complement your personal strengths with people who have strengths you don't.

Plus you have to accommodate the importance of delegation. If you have people who are better qualified than you in specific areas—and why wouldn't you?—their potential contribution will be realized only if you delegate to them the authority to do what you're paying them to do. This includes making decisions. If you aren't adequately delegating to people, it's either because you're personally uncomfortable or insecure about delegating authority, or they simply aren't competent. Any of these conditions will accrue to your detriment or demise at some point.

For best results, make the following your priorities:

- understanding the full complement of strengths required for your organization to be successful
- hiring for those strengths, without compromising or rationalizing
- configuring those strengths so the whole is greater than the sum of the parts, and yielding to the expertise of others when appropriate

Next, how do you make your decisions right?

Consider the following basic questions:

- What are the "conditions of satisfaction" the decision has to meet? What are the minimum goals the decision must satisfy? What is the absolute minimum required to solve the problem or deal effectively with the issue at hand?
- What is the absolute right answer? You'll never solve a problem or deal with an issue perfectly, but you have to start somewhere. If you know you're going to have to compromise, you're better off starting from the optimum point and making your compromises from there.
- Do your decisions culminate in the development of clear road maps for execution?
- Do you develop feedback systems to ensure that, on a regular basis, decisions get tested against actual events? Periodically and regularly ensure that decisions you made are still sound and that ensuing events or conditions don't torpedo you. Feedback systems help you adjust along the way.

Some cautionary notes:

- All decisions create unintended consequences. You might solve one problem and create three more. It's far better to anticipate possible consequences and develop a contingency plan than to be taken by surprise because you didn't confront foreseeable outcomes in advance.
- The effects of your decisions almost always appear in some remote future. Consider when the intended outcome(s) will probably occur. If, for example, you decide to increase prices, when (and how) will the incremental effect of that move impact your income statement?
- Make sure that your strategic decisions exploit your strengths and "starve" your weaknesses.

As you can see, a myriad of factors weigh in to help you make the right decisions—and make those decisions right. Keeping them top of mind will keep you out of trouble!

More Considerations

- Easy decisions don't exist. If the answer is obvious in advance, either a deeper inquiry is necessary or a decision isn't required in the first place.
- The people executing your decisions must buy in; they need to have their hearts in it. This is a real sticking point—one that can trip up both corporate executives and business owners.
- Realize that people must understand both the context and the content of your decisions.

Most executives have a hard time letting go. They get paid to make decisions. They also have a hard time envisioning how delegation can be accomplished effectively. So in the interest of time, they make too many decisions themselves that could have been made as well—or better—by others.

The problem is that people can disengage. High achievers stagnate and leave. Good performers die on the vine. Mediocre and poor performers stay because obedience is just fine with them.

Commitment vs. Compliance: Know the Difference

Most executives of both large and small companies wrestle with the structure of decision making in their corporate cultures.

I had to undertake that challenge myself as a senior executive in a financial services company. The CEO, who was semi-retired, had previously made the firm's important decisions, which he seemingly defined as almost *all* of the company's decisions, although he never explicitly articulated his criteria. Whenever someone else made a "bad" decision—i.e., any with which he disagreed—he punished the decision maker. Sometimes, that punishment was financial. Other times, he ignored the executive for a period of weeks to "send him a message." This may seem extreme, but it's true.

I worked for about three months to implement some necessary changes. Then the CEO confronted me after a former direct report of his and a new direct report of mine made what I agreed was a questionable decision. My response to that decision had been to meet with the executive to uncover his thought process and obtain his post-mortem assessment. The CEO responded by banging his fist on the desk and telling me what I should have done. "Rand," he said, "this is not a democracy."

My initial impulse was to respond in kind—but I didn't. Instead, I asked if we could meet that afternoon in his office to discuss the matter in greater depth. I figured we could both use a cooling-off period. I also needed time to craft an approach to our discussion that would yield a productive discussion and a reasonable outcome.

I prepared as best I could. Generally, my approach to these kinds of sessions was to ask the other person a series of questions; the answers would inexorably lead to a productive result. With this CEO, I started with, "I'm sure you believe that committed people perform better than compliant people, don't you?" When he answered "yes," I followed up with, "Do you believe that commitment is voluntary and that compliance, or obedience, is not?" Again, he answered "yes." I continued: "I sense that we believe the same thing. I also sense that you want the following: to preserve your decision-making options, to make sure that people who are making decisions are qualified to make them, and ensure those decisions are made at the appropriate level." He responded with a resounding "yes." We then dove into building a process for decision-making that would achieve all of those objectives.

Here are the issues: Most executives have a hard time letting go. They get paid to make decisions. They also have a hard time envisioning how delegation can be accomplished effectively. So in the interest of time, they make too many decisions themselves that could have been made as well—or better—by others.

The problem is that people can disengage. High achievers stagnate and leave. Good performers die on the vine. Mediocre and poor performers stay because obedience is just fine with them.

Continuum of Commitment

Peter Senge of *The Fifth Discipline* fame created a continuum to describe people's levels of dedication. "Grudging compliance" marks one end of this spectrum—that is, people do what's expected and no more; they're not really on board. In my experience, these people can also subvert organizational direction and strategies in subtle ways almost impossible to detect.

At the other end of the spectrum, "true commitment" indicates the highest level of dedication. At this end, people want to contribute aggressively to make things happen. They overcome obstacles with their energy and focus. In my experience, you can notice when organizations have hired and cultivated committed people. They crackle with energy. You can see their sparks of enthusiasm flying.

Commitment can't be mandated; it has to be earned, just like trust.

What does your organizational profile look like on the spectrum of dedication? Do you believe commitment makes a difference? How have you helped to create an environment in which people zealously commit? What are you willing to do about it going forward?

Plan your conversations. As the late business philosopher Jim Rohn once said, "Casual conversations are casualties."

Help People Solve Their Own Problems

As a senior corporate executive, I was especially proud of the degree to which people on every rung in every company where I worked had access to me. I didn't consider this access a burden because it was the source of my personal value proposition. If people needed to discuss a problem or an issue, they almost always felt comfortable using me as a resource, whether they reported directly to me or to someone four levels removed.

However, with accessibility comes responsibility as this story from my former life as a corporate executive illustrates.

I had just been promoted. Previously, I had about 200 people reporting directly or indirectly to me. When I woke up on Monday morning, my new team numbered about 1,500. I was livin' large.

In every job I had ever had—including this new one—I made a point of scheduling five total hours a week of one-on-one time with people in my organization(s) who didn't report directly to me. I did that for these reasons:

- To influence people's thinking, particularly around bigger strategic issues. People need to understand how what they do fits into the whole and why that matters.
- To set a tone and an implicit expectation for people reporting directly to me, i.e., that you need to know your people—their hopes, their fears, their motivations, their triggers.
- To enable me to peer into people's brains and get a sense of the quality of their thinking.
- To establish rapport and trust.

With that level of openness and engagement, however, comes an extremely high level of responsibility.

At the three-month mark of my new position, I had already conducted initial one-on-one discussions with about 150 people. Those meetings generally began with each person coming to my office, notepad in hand, eagerly anticipating sage words to be recorded. To break the ice, I went out of my way to inquire about each person's life and found it amazing how quickly the barriers came down.

My discussion with one young lady remains a vivid memory to this day. She entered my office red-faced and shaking like a volcano ready to erupt. I said, "You look concerned," and then I got up and fetched a bottle of water for her. Almost immediately, tears welled up in her eyes.

Then she did erupt. Using every vivid example she could think of, she spent about 45 minutes citing the ways in which her boss was a jerk. It was overwhelming. At the conclusion of her diatribe, I said, "So, you obviously have a problem, and if I allow you to leave now, we'll both have your problem."

She looked quizzical. I continued, "You see, if you leave my office right now, you're going to believe that because you shared this problem with me, I'm going to solve it for you. You'll expect that I'm actually going to do something to make your problem go away. Now's the time for you to tell me exactly *what* you'd like me to do about your problem."

At that point, I retrieved a box of Kleenex from my credenza. The welling in her eyes had transformed into tears on her cheeks.

"Well, I don't know," she replied.

I stood up, walked over to the white board on my office wall, and documented a list of alternatives that included my firing her boss, discussing the issues with her boss, and so on. She didn't like any of my ideas. Great—because I had no intention of actually *doing* any of them.

"So, here we are," I continued. "I fear that you've inferred that I made a commitment because I listened to your complaint and I'm the guy in charge. Yet, when I outlined specific, alternative actions, you wouldn't permit me to act on your behalf. So, we're left with two alternatives. Either you're just whining, which I know you wouldn't do because we've talked in the past as a group about the uselessness of whining, or *you* intend to do something about this and you came to me for support. I'm assuming that the latter is the case, and that you intend to take the reins yourself to solve your own problem. Is that right?"

"Well . . . yes," she replied timidly.

"Great! So here's what I'm going to do to support your bravery. Every Monday morning, I'll call you to see if you've actually had a discussion with your boss. This problem is between the two of you, and you need to solve it. I'm going to be relentless, so be forewarned. Hearing from me weekly will be a lot more of a pain to you than actually having the discussion you need to have with him. Okay, I think we're done here."

She shook my hand and left my office. I was certain she was thinking, "Yeah, right, he's going to call me every week!"

I did. For five Mondays in a row, I called her to remind her of her commitment. Each time she said she'd do something; each time she didn't . . . until week six.

I got a call from her. She sounded excited and asked if she could come to my office and discuss the matter. I said, "Fine," and she arrived a few minutes later with a HUGE, smug smile on her face.

"Well, my boss and I had the discussion," she started.

"Great! What happened?"

"Well, he was completely clueless. He had *no* idea I had a problem with him. Anyway, it was an emotional exchange; I could've done it better, but we agreed to get together again after I collect and compose myself."

I helped her brainstorm an approach. To this day, I have no idea if she used it. I do know that their relationship improved to the point of it being productive, although still never wonderful.

Word of this conversation spread throughout the company. The reputation I developed as a leader because of this incident carried me through many tough times. As a result, people gave me the benefit of the doubt, even when *I* wasn't sure they should.

Critical Communication Points for You as a Leader

- People will find out about your interactions, even the private ones. Make them count!
- To appear in charge, many leaders solve problems for people instead of helping people solve their own. Being the big kahuna doesn't mean being the "causer of all action" and "decider of all decisions." Your job is to enable people to function at a high level, independently and interdependently, but not dependently.
- Many leaders react to every interaction they have. Someone complains; they must do something. Don't be one of those. You'll create organizational schizophrenia.
- Plan your conversations. As the late business philosopher Jim Rohn once said, "Casual conversations are casualties." The words you choose, your body language, your tone will all be interpreted by people whose world views, perspectives, beliefs, and experiences are different than yours.
- Test for common understanding; make sure what you're saying is what other people are actually hearing. Here's an example. A CEO delivered a presentation at an all-associate meeting. At one juncture, to make a valid point, he said, "We're not here to make friends." With that statement, he intended to convey the notion that everyone needed to focus on the work at hand for the business to be successful. What people heard was, business and friendship are mutually exclusive (or maybe even contradictory). Bad news for his credibility.

When planning the nature and level of your own engagement with others, ask these questions:

- What do I want the other person/people to get out of this?
- What outcome will serve my needs as well?
- What outcome will preserve/advance the quality of my relationship with this person/these people?
- What result will better enable this person/these people to make an enthusiastic and relevant contribution to our company?

Notice the question I did *not* list: What outcome will demonstrate clearly that I'm da man?!

Remember, clear, direct, and consistent communication that helps associates solve their own problems will strengthen the entire organization.

If your associates are perceived by your current or prospective buyers as uncommitted or incapable, they will draw similar conclusions about your product and service quality.

Critical Reasons to Care About Your "Human Capital"

A question people ask me all the time is, "Why do company executives talk about people being an investment on the one hand and treat them as an expense on the other?"

People are treated as an expense because, from an accounting perspective, they are. That isn't to say they *ought* to be. But in strictly financial terms, people and everything to do with people—salaries, bonuses, benefits, development costs—are booked as expenses with other operating costs.

But regardless of accounting treatment and despite pressure to do otherwise, it's still prudent to think about human capital as an investment. Here are five reasons why:

1. Learning and deftness are the only sustainable competitive advantages. Product and service attributes come and go. Today's competitive advantage is tomorrow's competitive necessity. The ability of people—individually and in teams—to adjust on the run to changing competitive conditions is a company's only real enduring advantage.

2. Human capital is underutilized. Leaders of most companies aren't even aware of what their associates know.

3. People can easily move on. Competent people. Smart people. Creative people. Emotionally intelligent people. These kinds of people have options. If you don't value them by aligning their interests and strengths with your company's interests, developing their capacity to contribute, and rewarding their contributions—adios!

4. Historically, downsizing has been the primary refuge of uncreative minds groping for efficiency. "If we can have five people do the work of six, let's get rid of one," the thinking goes. I'm sure you've heard of survivors' guilt; I bet, however, you haven't consciously thought about survivors' anger, malice, and vitriol! The more that people observe irresponsible, episodic hiring and firing, the more company executives test their commitment.

5. From a training and development point of view, companies spend way too much time, money, and energy helping people develop in their areas of weakness. As a result, they haven't aligned strengths with organizational needs; rather, they've made weaknesses less weak. Bottom line: If your people are perceived by your current or prospective buyers as uncommitted or incapable, they will draw similar conclusions about your product and service quality.

What Four Big Questions Lead to Developing Your People?

To get answers that have high strategic leverage, you must ask big questions. For human capital to drive value creation, I suggest you begin with these:

1. What knowledge, skills, talents, and attributes does your organization require, and in what amounts and combinations, to create value for your targeted buyers?
2. How best can you recruit, select, develop, and leverage relevant knowledge, skills, talents, and attributes that create value for your targeted buyers?
3. What must you do to translate people's capabilities and commitment into performance?
4. What must you do to integrate each person's performance into a cohesive whole?

Thinking of your associates as an *expense* makes sense only from an accounting standpoint. People *are* the company. Wisdom dictates they be treated as an *investment*.

People have a burning desire to please the boss. Accordingly, when asked to make a commitment—even about something really important and on the spur of the moment—many executives will cave in to the pressure.

As a Leader, You *Have* to Understand the Power of Your Voice

During a strategy session with the executive team of a Fortune 200 company, the CEO reiterated his commitment to reduce the firm's expenses by 20 percent over the ensuing 24 months. During that session, he froze the senior VP of sales and marketing with an icy stare and speared him with the following inquiry: "John, you'll be able to hit your sales targets despite these expense reductions, won't you?" Apparently undaunted, John replied with his typical enthusiasm. "Sure—no problem!" After the meeting, I saw John in the hallway. He was, shall we say, less certain.

I later commented privately to the CEO that, after reviewing the assumptions in the company's sales plan, I believed the planned expense reduction would kill its chances of meeting its plan. His response? "I pay these people lots of money to overcome obstacles. John's a big boy. If he said they could do it, they'll do it."

They didn't do it. Here's why:

- Expense reduction always hits the bottom line quickly. The corresponding impact on the top line takes longer. As a result, executives usually rationalize that impact away. Many CEOs don't contemplate this. The great ones do.
- People have a burning desire to please the boss. Accordingly, when asked to make a commitment—even about something really important and on the spur of the moment—many executives will cave in to the pressure.
- Many CEOs don't recognize the power of their own voices. The great ones do.

How could this situation have been handled more effectively? The CEO could have said, "John, have you and your people contemplated the impact of these reductions on our sales plan?" When John responded in the affirmative, the follow-up could have gone like this: "The company's results are at stake here. We should all have a comfort level with the exact nature of that impact and the precise actions you have planned to overcome it. Let's set aside an hour or two this afternoon (assuming John is ready) to discuss this."

How would you have handled this problem? Would you have recognized that to engender commitment and enthusiasm among the team members, you would need to deal with the reality and complexity of this situation? Would you have been willing to subordinate your ego to get to the right answers and increase everyone's confidence?

Are you one of the great ones—or are you willing to be?

When performance issues are neglected, both the company and the person pay. A failure to be candid can easily hurt someone's chances of being or becoming an effective contributor. The flip side of the coin is the development of superior achievers. We have to identify those in a systematic way and reward them in a more substantial way.

Capability, Confidence, and Commitment: Goal of Performance Feedback

Decades ago, Stephen R. Covey recommended that we "start with the end in mind" as one of his seven habits. Covey's book *The 7 Habits of Highly Successful People* has stood the test of time because of its practical relevance. Many so-called "how to make your life better" books espouse lofty, elusive, and sometimes metaphysical concepts. *The 7 Habits* not only explains *what* to do, it tells you *how* to do it.

That said, many of us read an author's exhortations convinced that we're already doing the right things, even when we're not. No better example exists than organizational leaders who, by definition, must rely upon others' efforts and accomplishments for their own success, but who cultivate compliance and conformity rather than confidence, capability, and commitment.

Take this example: After five years as a super salesman with a Fortune 500 pharmaceutical and consumer goods company, Steve accepted a position as a division sales manager with a similarly large pharmaceutical company.

Steve wanted to hit the ground running. He gathered his new team of high achievers together on his first day and gave them the Knute Rockne "win one for the Gipper" speech, impressing his new boss and his own team with his energy and eloquence. During the next few months, Steve traveled with his sales people individually to demonstrate his closing technique. In so doing, he personally closed a lot of sales. This guy was a rainmaker extraordinaire. Yet when Steve turned the reins over to his sales team, they flopped.

Steve believed that demonstrating his closing skill would provide sufficient inspiration to propel his sales team to success. It didn't. Inspiration does not guarantee success. If Steve had really thought about Covey's advice—starting with the end in mind—he might have concluded that what he really wanted was a capable, confident, and committed sales team. Were those ends achieved by Steve's demonstration of personal selling ability? No way.

Here's How to Do It

During a talk I once gave as a Fortune 500 executive to my staff, I outlined criteria for what I believed every associate deserved. They go a long way toward developing capability and engendering confidence and commitment. Here's that part of the presentation:

"Managers must work with you to convey in advance what's expected of you, how your contribution and performance fits into the whole, and how that performance will be measured. We need committed people, not compliant people. Committed people make independent decisions. Committed people make aggressive contributions. Compliant people—those who just do what they're told—don't challenge convention; they simply obey and can't or won't make the kind of contribution that's necessary. We cannot assess how effective we are as managers doing that. It can only be measured by whether we achieve planned results as seen in the energy, tenacity, enthusiasm, courage, and fortitude of the people who make results happen.

"A healthy environment encourages people to achieve their own aspirations as well as the company's. Solid managers place a lot of emphasis on that because, while the enterprise is responsible for creating opportunities, people must be prepared when those opportunities arise.

"We have to limit our tolerance of marginal or poor performance. We don't currently do an adequate job of distinguishing levels of performance. Part of that is because we don't do a great job of precisely defining expectations. Some managers kid themselves into believing that time will correct performance problems or that being fair means being indulgent. We have to work with people to improve, but we can't dodge our responsibility to be aggressive performance managers. By indulging or, in some cases, rewarding anemic performance, we're condoning it. High fliers will not work where poor performance is tolerated.

"When performance issues are neglected, both the company and the person pay. A failure to be candid—sensitive and empathetic but candid—can easily hurt someone's chances of being or becoming an effective contributor. The flip side of the coin is the development of superior achievers. We have to identify them in a systematic way and reward them in a more substantial way."

Managing Performance: 3 Steps

I suggest following three steps for managing performance, then developing, implementing, and reviewing it. The steps are:

1. **Plan at all levels.** Planning is a process of identifying and linking "ends" and "means" at every organizational level. In that way, organizational action plans become departmental objectives; departmental action plans to achieve those objectives then become individual objectives; and so on, in a way that's called "cascading."
2. **Hold annual objective-setting discussions.** They should include all people, face to face, and one on one.
3. **Conduct regular face-to-face performance reviews.** They involve discussing individual results vs. the plan, setting up corrective actions, and determining prospects for future assignments.

As a consultant and coach, I've worked with many executives who demonstrate a belief that at senior levels, managers should be self-sufficient, immune from the need for development discussions, and emotionally inoculated from criticism. That's simply not the case.

Look at your own development and performance management activities with those who report to you. Do your actions demonstrate the end you want—that is, cultivating commitment, confidence, and capability rather than mandating conformance and compliance? If they don't, reconsider your approach now.

As an organizational leader, you hire the people, you establish the standards, you set the expectations, and you ensure accountability. If you're doing those things, there's a good chance planned results will happen. If you aren't, they won't. Quite simple.

If Your People *Are* Performing, It's Them; If They *Aren't*, It's You

If you lead any size of organization—from a two-person start-up to a Fortune 500 company—and your people are achieving planned results regularly, congratulations to them; they're doing a great job. If, however, they're not regularly achieving planned results, then *you* are not doing *your* job!

As an organizational leader, you hire the people, you establish the standards, you set the expectations, and you ensure accountability. If you're doing those things, there's a good chance planned results will happen. If you aren't, they won't. Quite simple.

I got a call from a senior leader of a Fortune 100 (I'll call him Fred) ostensibly to work with one of his direct reports, John. As Fred told me the story, John had a "rough engagement style." For those not tuned into corporate jargon, that meant John didn't play well with others.

At the appointed time, I visited separately with Fred and John to discuss the issue and get their separate "takes" on how they saw the problem. As it turned out, my bringing up the issue with John was the first he'd heard of it; not one discussion with Fred had happened—ever!

When I raised the point with Fred, he gazed at me in disbelief. "I'm not going to have that discussion with John," he responded. "He might get angry or dispirited!"

I kept my dismay to myself. I am, after all, a trained professional. Instead, I calibrated my response and tone both to get to the point and make sure Fred heard it.

"So, Fred," I began, "what I'm hearing you say is that dealing with this issue will be *my* problem, not yours." I really expected a response something like, "Not at all, Rand. I didn't know how to deal with this, so I was hoping you could help me as well as John."

Not quite!

Instead, Fred responded with "that's right." I took a deep breath and shared with him the story of another of my clients, a Fortune 100 CEO who spends an average of 500 hours a year reviewing the performance and development of the top 200 managers in his company. Fred then asked, "When does he have time to do his job?" My disbelief deepened.

I won't continue with this story; you get the picture. I become re-aggravated just thinking that this highly compensated caveman actually believed he didn't own any part of his people's performance and development.

You don't have to lapse into "terminal niceness" to be effective. Face it. You can't possibly achieve success as an organizational leader without doing these things. You won't get results; you won't get performance; you won't get respect; and ultimately (quite frankly), you won't get to keep your job (I hope).

This isn't a tangential matter; it strikes at the heart of performance and represents both a huge opportunity and problem for most leaders. If you can honestly say you currently do a good job on these matters, congratulations. You're in the minority. If not, you're missing a primary opportunity for leadership leverage.

Some people view the skill of captivating an audience as mere form over true substance. But don't kid yourself. People subconsciously draw conclusions about you based on the deftness of your delivery at the podium. And a powerful presentation sells them on your subject.

9 Steps to Delivering a Killer Presentation

If you're a business owner, corporate executive, or manager—or you aspire to any of these positions—it's essential that you be able to deliver powerful, compelling presentations.

Some people view the skill of captivating an audience as mere form over true substance. But don't kid yourself. People subconsciously draw conclusions about you based on the deftness of your delivery at the podium. And a powerful presentation sells them on your subject.

To sharpen your skills and get the results you want, follow these 9 steps to delivering a killer presentation:

1. Start with the end in mind. Define the objective and work backward.
2. Use enough logic for the listener to justify an emotional decision. Pick up some pointers from *The Pyramid Principle* by Barbara Minto. This book will help you better employ logic in crafting your presentations—especially when you want to persuade the audience to make a decision or take action.

3. Keep in mind that all business is show business and all presentations are sales presentations.

4. Focus on benefits, not features. People are more interested in solving *their* problems than knowing the details of *your* solution. First identify and recognize their problem and the "pain" they're in. Then show how you can eliminate it.

5. Craft your presentation in the following order:

    - WHY should they care? If your audience can't determine within a minute or two why they should care about what you're saying, you've lost them. Again, define their problem and acknowledge their pain first.

    - WHAT are you going to do to solve their problem?

    - HOW are you going to solve it?

    - WHAT IF they decide to say "yes"? Describe how their situation will be better and help them feel the relief.

6. Be a good storyteller. Paint word pictures. If you're using PowerPoint, invoke the 10/20/30 rule when possible: 10 slides, 20 minutes, 30-point typeface. (Thanks to business guru and author Guy Kawasaki for this rule.)

7. Of Cicero, people said, "What a great orator." Of Demosthenes, they said, "Let us march!" Work on the craft of public speaking until you're at least comparable to Cicero—but aspire to the status of Demosthenes.

8. Be authentic in engaging your audience, whether it's one person or one thousand.

9. Remember the power and necessity of delivering dynamite presentations as a leader. Spend the time and effort required to become a superb orator and the dividends will far outweigh the costs.

In the 1990s, the word "empowerment" created confusion and angst for those looking to balance equitable power dispersion and effective decision-making. Managers' desire to either appease their workforce or desperately cling to their own power had undesirable results: abdication or even more entrenched autocracy.

Effective Delegation Says It; Empowerment Does Not

I dislike buzzwords. They simplify complex phenomena to a degree that frequently degrades the original concept. One example is "re-engineering." Michael Hammer and James Champy coined this phrase to describe a "radical redesign of business processes to achieve dramatic improvements in quality, service, and productivity." Hammer's article in the *Harvard Business Review* titled "Re-engineering—Don't Automate, Obliterate," was appropriately greeted with awe. Many great companies got on the re-engineering bandwagon and implemented the concept productively. Within a couple of years, however, the word "re-engineering" became synonymous with layoffs. No radical redesign. No improvement in service.

In the 1990s, the word "empowerment" became another such word, creating confusion and angst for those looking to balance equitable power dispersion and effective decision-making. Managers' desire to either appease their workforce or desperately cling to their own power had undesirable results: abdication or even more entrenched autocracy.

I make great efforts not to use the "e" word anymore because of differing definitions that reside in the heads of listeners. Instead, I employ the phrase "effective delegation." These four elements make up what I call effective delegation: authority, autonomy, responsibility, and accountability. Let me expand on them.

1. **Authority** concerns the parameters within which a manager will allow an individual or team to make decisions and take action. Undefined authority frequently leads to second-guessing and turmoil.
2. **Autonomy** means freedom from oversight. That can only exist to the degree that the manager's anxiety allows. Former Intel CEO Andrew Grove coined the phrase "task-relevant maturity" to frame thinking about both authority and autonomy. He believed that they must be earned by demonstrating skills and solid past performances related to specific tasks. While this logic may seem obvious, its implications are rarely considered in practice.
3. **Responsibility** relates to the specifics of a person's job. For example, an effective manager would not delegate strategic information technology decisions to a 25-year-old salesperson with no technology background.
4. **Accountability** is a word that gets thrown around indiscriminately. Accountability refers to consequences—in an organizational context, the consequences of decisions and actions. Indeed, without consequences, accountability does not exist. Depending on the circumstances and the performance, they can be either positive or negative. For example, a sales person's consequence for exceeding his or her sales plan may include a huge bonus or increased commission. A project manager's consequence for missing target dates and cost objectives might be the loss of his or her job. The greater the

degree of delegation, the more precise and unyielding the accountability needs to be.

When delegating, over-simplifying can be deadly if managers view competence as an all-or-nothing proposition. If John is labeled "competent" in one area, then it's frequently and erroneously assumed he's totally competent in all areas. Conversely, if John is not competent in a particular area, he's mistakenly considered totally incompetent in all areas.

Remember, a manager's success requires identifying areas of unique competence and deploying them productively. Expansive, well-thought-out delegation is a critical component.

The legitimate value of the product or service exists only in the buyer's perception. *That means the buyer—the potential user or user—is the only one who can assign value.*

- **Durability.** This is concerned with how long the product will last and how that duration affects a particular user or potential customer.
- **Serviceability.** This aspect consists of the speed, competence, and courtesy involved in repairing the product or service.
- **Aesthetics.** This subjective dimension includes the look, feel, taste, sound, or smell of a product. Is it pleasing to the senses?
- **Perceived quality.** This component has been referred to as the "halo effect." It means the impression a customer develops of a product or service based on experience or hearsay. This impression radiates to other products and services from that company whether or not it's accurate across the board. For example, 25 years ago I owned a car that developed body rot at 12,000 miles and couldn't start in cold weather from the outset. I have never since bought a car made by that manufacturer.

Some of these eight dimensions apply more to certain products or services than others; all require further breakdown into relevant components. For example, within the reliability dimension, consider the billing process for a financial services company. Three reliability measures worth considering are (1) mean time to first error, (2) mean time between errors, and (3) error rate per number of bills issued.

Addressing All Dimensions of Value

Many companies are obsessed with expense reduction rather than overall value creation. But to remain competitive, a company must address all relevant dimensions of value. This requires:

- appropriate measures and rewards; what gets rewarded gets done.
- an explicit understanding of the precise needs and values of specific customers and segments.
- organizational and individual competencies aligned with the dimensions of value important to specific customers and segments.

Today, brand development and management has become "front and center" because branding has a lot to do with *value creation.* Brand management concerns the total relationship between the company and the customer. It involves how the company portrays its products and services and how the customer perceives them. Many companies dedicate their resources to how they portray their products and services. However, effective brand management and developing brand equity require an obsession with value creation. That means reversing these priorities and focusing on customer perception of value—the crucial factor that sells.

To succeed beyond survival, you have to offer your customers exceptional value. *To stand out and be the talk of the town, you also have to focus on providing* unforeseeable value. *How successful do you want to be?*

From Basic to Beyond Exceptional—What Value Do You Create?

Business guru Peter Drucker was right when he said, "The purpose of a business is to create and keep a customer." It follows, therefore, that the primary objective of any business is *to create value to attract and maintain customers*. Seems obvious, but let's look deeper.

Value creation exists on four ascending levels: basic, expected, exceptional, and unforeseeable. If you want to be a long-term player in business, you need to understand these levels and think about their implications for you.

1. *Basic value* allows you into the game. Thus, if you're in the business of new car sales, then having cars to sell provides this basic value. More formally defined, it's the level of value that meets the limited expectations of the "mass-market" buyer.
2. *Expected value* is what you deliver once you define your "targeted" buyers—your market segment. It's the level of value that meets at least the minimum expectations of those buyers.

3. *Exceptional value* exceeds what your targeted buyers need or expect.

4. *Unforeseeable value* features innovative elements or exaggerated levels of value that haven't even been contemplated by the buyer.

Let me summarize this way: To exist, your business must create *basic value* to attract customers. To survive, you must create *expected value* for your targeted buyers. To succeed beyond survival, you have to offer your customers *exceptional value*. To stand out and be the talk of the town, you also have to focus on providing *unforeseeable value*.

How successful do you want to be?

What Level of Value Means

When determining the level of value to deliver to your customers, keep in mind the following:

- Value has both quality and cost components.
- Anything that doesn't create value creates waste.
- Buyers' expectations evolve relative to:
    - what's available in the market,
    - the longevity of their relationship with you, and
    - their level of satisfaction with you.

Remember, the only reason for customer feedback is to help you determine where you need to improve. If it's employed for any other reason, it's useless. So if your customer feedback consistently validates your performance, you're either asking the wrong questions or asking them the wrong way.

The One and Only Reason for Customer Feedback

A while ago, I had new windows installed in my home by a large, nationwide provider who both made the product and did the installation work. When my wife and I decided to go with this firm, we met with the salesman to sign the paperwork, select a date, and (most important to him) provide a deposit check.

Just before the close of our meeting, the salesman mentioned the survey the company sends customers to complete after the installation. Here's the kicker: What he really wanted to tell us was that only one rating—the highest one—would be acceptable to the company. If we evaluated its performance in any lower category, one or more people either wouldn't get their annual raise or their bonus, or they might be fired.

Can you predict my response? I chose to leave the histrionics out of it. Instead, I peppered the salesman with questions such as:

- How will you improve if you don't know where you need to make adjustments?

- What's the point of people being deluded into thinking they're doing a great job if they're not?

I could tell by the look on his face that he viewed my questions as secondary to the real point—making him look good to his company.

Remember this: The only reason for customer feedback is to help you determine where you need to improve. If it's employed for any other reason, it's useless. So if your customer feedback consistently validates your performance, you're either asking the wrong questions or asking them in the wrong way.

What should you do? Dig deeper, celebrate new insights, and become vigilant about continuous improvement.

If you actually invite and directly address all buyer feedback—especially the stingers—it can make the difference between prosperity and bankruptcy depending on how you deal with it.

Your Response to Customers Can Make or Break You

It's natural to wince at unfavorable feedback, even when you profess that you want it. Some people take criticism personally and either find a way to blame the provider or create a reason that any transgression is an anomaly. However, if you actually invite and directly address all buyer feedback—especially the stingers—it can make the difference between prosperity and bankruptcy *depending on how you deal with it.*

You'll find the following personal examples instructive.

Several years ago, I received an email with an attached PowerPoint presentation from a person I'd never met. It seems he and a business associate had made a guaranteed reservation at a hotel in Houston. They arrived late at night, and the front desk clerk had given their room to a walk-in. A lengthy discussion ensued between these two men and the clerk. Bottom line: The clerk had blown it but concocted excuse after excuse indicating that these guys were culpable because of their late arrival. A couple of days later, these irate customers crafted a lengthy, humorous PowerPoint presentation and emailed it to both the clerk and the hotel manager.

Hang on; that's not the end of it. They also sent a copy of their presentation to a thousand of their friends, associates, and acquaintances—including me. I became curious about how many people had eventually received the PowerPoint, so I called a few of them and asked, "How many people did *you* send it to?" and "Would you please share a few of their names?" Then I called a few of *those* recipients and asked the same questions. Here's the killer: According to my conservative estimate, about 50,000 people eventually received a copy of this anti-customer service presentation.

With today's electronic connectivity, news (both good and bad) travels far and fast!

But let's look at the flip side of this customer service feedback coin.

A few years ago, bad winter storms caused our family to lose a number of shingles on our cedar shake roof. A neighbor had a restoration company over to do work at his home, so I asked the workman about getting a roofer to look at our roof. He recommended Gene Phifer with Phifer Construction in Montgomery County, Maryland. I called Gene, he came out, walked the roof, and said it was okay but he would look at it the following year to reassess its condition.

For the next couple of years, I called Gene in the fall. Each time, he walked the roof, reassessed its condition, and repeated that while the shingles were getting dry, the underlying roofing paper was still good. He never charged for this service nor exploited our ignorance. When we finally decided to replace the roof, I called him for an estimate. I also got estimates from two other companies and completed my reference checks. *Everyone* I contacted raved about

Gene's service. He had even maintained one elderly man's roof that he hadn't installed. We decided to hire him.

After we signed the agreement, Gene showed up when he said he would, his workers were pleasant, and they cleaned up after they finished the job. Sometime after that, we had severe storms and experienced problems where water seeped in. I called Gene and he came to our home within *two* hours! He boarded up the area until the rain subsided and before long, returned to correct the problems. He followed up to be sure the corrections remained secure. Later, he had his painter repaint water-stained areas (including areas that existed before his roofing job). Because of our experience and recommendation, he has done at least five of our neighbors' roofs.

Gene Phifer is not Jack Welch nor Peter Drucker. He doesn't have a Harvard MBA. But he does have an innate sense of the lifetime value of a customer. Do you?

What These Examples Demonstrate

- In the information age, word travels quickly and broadly.
- Good marketing doesn't primarily involve focus groups and systematic feedback but, rather, keeping every commitment you make. The rule of thumb? Under commit and over deliver, not the other way around.
- A "can-do" obsession can overcome minor lapses in quality or service. The clerk at the hotel in this example treated his customers with antagonism instead of conciliation. Contrast that with Gene the roofer who knows that the real test of product and service quality came after the original work was done.

- Carefully consider and even solicit feedback from your customers. The more critical the feedback, the better.
- The key is to respond immediately to negative comments with a positive approach that strives to resolve complaints to the customer's satisfaction. And yes, going "above and beyond" will go far to spread your good reputation.

A colleague's comment sparked a whole new perspective for me—that is, a realization that our society actually functions on four economies. I believe both business and personal success depend on recognizing that.

Value Creation: Where Does It Live Within the Four Economies?

I recently had a discussion with a person who'd been a senior staffer in a federal government agency and became a Fortune 100 executive officer, his first job in industry. He commented that he'd worked much harder in government than in private industry, but believed "hours worked" was a more accurate measure of one's contribution than "value created." "People in business ask too many questions," he said. "They need to understand the reasons and context for their actions. I don't get that."

This comment sparked a whole new perspective for me—that is, a realization that our society actually functions on four economies. I believe both business and personal success depend on recognizing that.

I describe these four economies this way:

- *The entrepreneurial economy*—is comprised of closely held companies. The business owners and entrepreneurs who lead them require buyers to purchase their products and services to achieve professional and personal success. It's obvious that creating value for their buyers every day is a must.

- *The intrapreneurial economy*—describes companies that have grown big and matured. While others go to seed, these large, talented organizations remain competitively vibrant, focusing their resources on value creation. Those who work in these firms retain their competitive vigor.
- *The corpor-ocratic economy*—is represented by firms that have become bloated, stodgy, and internally focused. The people who work in these organizations have developed in a similar way.
- *The bureaucratic economy*—is comprised of government agencies and soon-to-be-extinct companies. Their purpose, plans, people, processes, and procedures focus inwardly.

Many individuals have their hearts in one economy and their feet in another. The implications of this can be highly dysfunctional for them and their place of work. In practical terms, that means if you're a business owner or a corporate leader, your success could be driven by actions like these:

- identifying where your organization needs to be on the continuum of four economies,
- assuring that your own behavior as well as your organizational mechanisms comport with the requirements for prosperity, and
- recruiting people with a work orientation that will drive your success—an especially critical factor. If, for example, your firm, in its infancy, requires significant market share growth, then hiring risk-averse, inwardly focused people will not take your company to the "promised land." Neither will entrepreneurial people if you confine them with bureaucratic constraints.

Many organizational leaders erroneously believe that either the right strategy, intelligent people, vigilant execution, or an entrepreneurial disposition is sufficient for achieving success. Wrong. Bottom line: Succeeding takes alignment, evolution, and constant reassessment of all these elements in an economic structure focused on value creation.

Companies of any size—whether they are Fortune 500 manufacturers or single-location yoga studios—need to operate with a big dose of competitive paranoia. The terrain constantly changes, so you can either eat *lunch or* be *lunch.*

Look Around: Are Your Competitors Eating You for Lunch?

What do bookstores, movies theaters, and grocery stores have in common? They all must navigate a competitive terrain that is vastly changing. The following three examples provide insights you can extrapolate for your business, whether you work for a Fortune 500 company or operate solo.

I was standing in an unacceptably long line waiting to pay for my purchase at one of the country's mega-booksellers. I counted 10 people in front of me, six people behind me, one salesperson working a register, and one manager who stood fulfilling the role of disengaged observer. After paying for my purchase, I asked if I could have a word with him. He agreed.

Anticipating a tirade, he began apologizing for his staffing shortage, but that's not what I wanted to talk about. I began, "Sir, I'm in the business of helping executives, entrepreneurs, and companies create and sustain success. I'm always interested in the changing competitive environment and the pressure it exerts on established businesses. May I ask you a couple of questions?" I could see the blood flow return to his face as he answered, "Yes, of course."

"If I can buy this book (pointing to my purchase) for twenty to thirty percent less money at Amazon, why should I buy it here?" His response—and this is no lie or exaggeration—was "personal service." I asked him to explain what he meant by that. He stared at me as if I had a third eye in the middle of my forehead and finally replied, "Why don't you just return your book and buy it from Amazon!"

Now *there's* personal service.

Two Compelling Examples

An article I read about distribution in the motion picture industry speculated about the potential irrelevance of movie theaters. I remember an additional piece that included comments from Mark Cuban, former Internet music mogul, owner of the NBA basketball team Dallas Mavericks, and aspiring film industry tycoon. In his discussion with more "seasoned" film industry marketing executives, he'd wondered aloud if it might be a sage move to release films into theaters and on DVD simultaneously.

Curious, I decided to pursue my own inquiry into the subject and called an executive with a large theater chain I knew to meet for lunch. I asked him about Cuban's comments. He dismissed them as irrelevant speculation, which sounded to me like a rationalization for the status quo. I followed his comment with this question: "If movies and DVDs of the movies were released simultaneously, which groups of people would continue to come to your theaters and why?" He immediately became less cordial and the decibel level of his voice rose. "Look," he said, freezing me with a glare, "it's just not going to happen!"

Are you detecting a similar theme here?

A few years ago, the parent of a large mid-Atlantic grocery store chain decided it could no longer compete without making dramatic strategic changes. Its expenses were too high to compete with low-cost providers and its level of differentiation wasn't sufficient to go head-to-head with the Whole Foods or Trader Joes of the world. As strategy guru Michael Porter would put it, this chain was "stuck in the middle."

Its decision-makers opted to incrementally reduce costs, resulting in staffing reductions and increased automated checkout technology. Now shoppers can find precious little help, and the quality of the produce has slipped discernibly. This store remains stuck.

I queried the store manager about the changes. In response, he railed against the corporation and its remote, out-of-touch leadership, and pined for the "good old days." When I asked about the company's direction, he was clueless.

Clearly, indifferent service and poor quality had accompanied the cost reductions. I have since learned that the rate of return to the holding company from this business has since deteriorated significantly. Their competitors are eating them for lunch!

Keep These Points in Mind

- Companies of any size—whether they are Fortune 500 manufacturers or single-location yoga studios—need to operate with a big dose of competitive paranoia. The terrain constantly changes, so you can either *eat* lunch or *be* lunch.
- Success can be insidious if it causes complacency. Never be satisfied with the status quo if you want to grow.
- Any company's value proposition needs to be precise and quantifiable. Too many firms leave their strategy in the stratosphere—lofty, abstract, and unsupported by fact. Remember, hallucination is not the same as vision.
- Ask these strategic questions consistently and constantly to keep up with change:
  - Who are we?
  - Where are we today?
  - Who and where do we want to be?
  - By when?
  - How will we get there?
  - Who is going to do what and by when?
  - How are we doing and what are we doing about it?

Draconian cost reductions are usually the first recourse of uncreative minds—and they're almost always accompanied by insistence that quality won't suffer. Some companies pull this off; most don't.

To people anywhere who decide to plant their feet and work for productive change—Bravo! Find other like-minded people to provide you with the courage to continue the fight. Incubate ideas; initiate independent action; take risks; build the company you want.

Denny Flanagan—a Customer Service Champion

I'm infinitely interested in certain things and completely disinterested in others, which includes anything mechanical; you'll find little middle ground with me.

When I put my key into the ignition of my car, something happens to make it start that I don't have to understand. And I love watching good TV programs, but I don't care how the picture gets into my TV. However, show me a customer service champion and I'm all over it. I'm completely curious about people who make a difference.

This brings me to Captain Dennis J. Flanagan of United Airlines. Here's what happened that piqued my interest.

My wife and I were flying to Arizona to spend a week in Sedona. Our Denver-bound flight was to leave from Baltimore on United Airlines. About 30 minutes before our scheduled departure, we sat at the gate waiting to board when the door to the Jetway opened. The United captain emerged, strode to the ticket counter, and grabbed the microphone. Based on my substantial flying experience, a variety of possible scenarios bombarded my brain—none of them good!

Then this captain began speaking. "Good morning, ladies and gentlemen. I'm your captain, Denny Flanagan." He went on to describe the weather we anticipated and our route. Then he said, "We're flying a Boeing 757 this morning. If you have any questions during our flight about the aircraft or flight, I'll be happy to answer them. Our plane this morning is in great shape." A long pause ensued, then, "And *I'm* in good shape." The passengers chuckled. "By the way," he continued, "this is my first flight." Silence . . . "Today!" he added with a grin.

Great. He does schtick! He's a pilot I can relate to.

Among the waiting passengers, I could see their moods quickly change like a wave. They hadn't previously appeared anxious or worried, just indifferent or tired. After that announcement, they seemed jovial and eager to board.

We wondered what would happen next. Jimmy Buffet with a parrot? A conga line?

As we began boarding, Captain Flanagan stood at the door to the plane handing out cards with a 757 pictured on one side and a description of the aircraft on the other. Greeting him, I mentioned I was an executive coach and consultant, and that I published a monthly newsletter. I said I'd like to write something about his congeniality and gave him my business card. He replied that he'd love to talk at some point.

An hour into our flight, Anne, the purser, spoke over the intercom saying, "Good morning, ladies and gentlemen. We here at United believe travel should be fun. So Captain Flanagan is raffling off discounted tickets on United."

Wait a minute, now we're having a raffle? What's next? Karaoke?

She continued, "On your cocktail napkin, please write down the reason you chose United for your air travel. I'll then draw four napkins and read the responses. Those people will each receive a coupon worth a discount on a future United flight."

The raffle concluded and I didn't win. But a few minutes later, Anne came down the aisle with one of Captain Flanagan's business cards. On the back was this note: "Mr. Golletz, You are a valued customer and your business is greatly appreciated. Please let me know how we can exceed your expectations. Also, could you wait for me after the flight?" Signed, "Capt. Denny."

I couldn't meet him because of a tight connection in Denver, so I asked Anne to tell him I'd call him after my Sedona vacation, saying I was eager to know more about him. Before taking my response to Denny in the cockpit, she told me what she knew about this unusual and extraordinary guy:

- He institutes the raffle on every flight and posts the cocktail napkin responses where United staffers can read them.
- He has a large number of copies of a coffee-table-sized book on United's history and presents them to United associates who respond to customers in exceptional ways.
- He handwrites personal thank you notes on the back of his business cards to every first-class passenger on every one of his flights.
- He provides his personal credit card to unaccompanied minors on his flights so they can use the in-flight phone to call home.
- One of Denny's co-pilots, Buck Wyndham (how's that for a pilot's name?), was so impressed that he asked Denny if

he could record him for several days after the brass okayed the idea. The video recording was then used for training at the company.

When I got home from that vacation, I spoke to Denny and a number of people close to him. My primary question was, "What created this dedication to customers?" Denny said, "I do it because it's my job." Not a guy prone to self-congratulatory behavior. His wife, Terri, told me he has a profound sense of duty and loyalty that endures despite adverse circumstances. His associate Bud Potts, another United pilot, couldn't explain this quality in Denny. He expressed his admiration for both who Denny is and what he does.

Keep On Learning from Captain Denny

What have I learned (or reaffirmed) from my experience with Captain Denny? Here are three conclusions:

1. For years, United Airlines has gone through lots of well-documented challenges. Providing a bright spot amid the fray is a leader who demonstrates resilience, persistence, tenacity, a love of people, loyalty, and dedication. Where he got it isn't as important as that he has it. Character counts!
2. People follow examples rather than orders. Frequently, Denny preaches the word of customer service to other United associates. They listen to him because his actions mirror his words. He's consistent and authentic. He reaffirms what he says with what he does.
3. When faced with challenging times and circumstances, we have choices. We can focus on the good with a positive attitude or whine about the way things are and harbor resentment. You've probably heard it before and I'll say it again: *Resentment is tantamount to drinking poison and expecting someone else to*

die. I know people at United who want the company to fail because of deep-seated animosity and their need to prove themselves right. At the risk of appearing simplistic, I say, "Find something else to do with your life!"

When times get tough, people throw in the towel and leave out of frustration. To those at United and other firms who have confronted similar challenges and gotten out, I say, "Sometimes leaving is the right answer—for both the organization and the person. Better to leave than seethe."

To people anywhere who decide to plant their feet and work for productive change—Bravo! Find other like-minded people to provide you with the courage to continue the fight. Incubate ideas; initiate independent action; take risks; build the company you want.

To everyone, but most particularly the executive managers of United, what can you learn from this story and how can you leverage that lesson? Will you have the courage and smarts to place your bets on people like Denny Flanagan?

P.S. I first wrote about Denny in my monthly newsletter in 2005. Since then, others have also noticed his amazing qualities. For example, he has appeared on TV network shows "This Morning" and "Good Morning America" and has been featured in a page-one story in the *Wall Street Journal.* In an industry that desperately needs heroes, Denny joins pilot Sully Sullenberger (of "put the plane down in the Hudson River" fame) as a guy worth emulating. I'm proud that Denny and I have become good friends. When he's in D.C. or Baltimore, we still have dinner together. (Come to think of it, Denny, you owe me a meal.)

How can you make sure people in your company "get it" and delight your customers? Going that extra mile can transform your entire journey into one of gratifying success.

Service After the Sale: Sellers Who "Get It"

You just closed a huge deal; another buyer has decided that "you da man." Time to cash that check and move on to the next opportunity.

Not so fast, Mr. Wonderful! You've neglected Rule #1 in marketing. Customer expectations begin just as your attentiveness starts to subside. The real business of selling begins *after* you've made the sale!

Some companies get it; others don't.

Chad Older of Washington, D.C., was flying over America on Southwest Airlines. His father-in-law called carrier representatives and asked them to inform Chad that his pregnant wife had just gone into labor—six weeks early. When Chad landed to make his connection, an emissary from Southwest was waiting. She told him the situation and whisked him off to a gate so he could fly home in lieu of going to his original destination. The Southwest representative told Chad that the rebooked flight was full, but that they would "provide sufficient incentives" for a passenger to volunteer his or her seat. Despite Chad's insisting on paying for his new flight, Southwest gave him the new ticket *for free!*

Once the family got the new baby home, Chad wrote Southwest a thank you note. Lo and behold, Southwest sent a gift to his baby. (Thanks to *The Washington Post* for this story.)

Southwest gets it!

Another example: I had just bought a suit at Nordstrom—a dark brown, spectacular-looking Hart, Schaffner and Marx Gold Trumpeter. A few days later, I wore my new suit for the first time. "Yes, you're lookin' good!" my mirror told me.

Distracted by my own "studliness," I walked into my garage to hop into my SUV and tore one of the suit sleeves on the rear windshield wiper. No one was around to blame—I looked. So I called my Nordstrom salesman, Rudolph Ruiz, and asked if the company's tailor could reweave the material to make the tear less obvious. Rudolph asked me to bring the suit in.

After I dropped off the suit, he later called to tell me that Nordstrom's tailor had determined the damage was irreparable. However, he had an alternative solution and asked me to stop in to discuss it. I wondered what he had in mind until I arrived at Nordstrom. He unveiled a selection of suits from which I could pick a replacement. *For free!*

I was speechless. Nordstrom had no complicity in my stupidity, and yet here was my salesman volunteering a replacement—gratis! I considered the options he'd selected for me (which included a Joseph Abboud and a $1,200 Hickey-Freeman), made my selection, and got out before Rudolph could change his tune.

Nordstrom gets it!

On another personal but less complimentary note, I was running late to catch a plane out of Dulles Airport in Washington D.C. I'd just passed through security and was about to board a shuttle bus when I realized I had no idea which gate I was going to. I'd forgotten to check the monitors before taking off my shoes, shedding my jewelry, and unpacking my laptop to pass through the security checkpoint. So I leaned back to address a trusted associate of the government security agency TSA, explained my predicament, and asked where I might find a monitor. He looked at me with a blank expression and said, "It's not my job to make your life easier." He then turned away and continued his business.

A lot of systemic reasons cause government workers, on the whole, to be less responsive to their "customers" than people in the private sector tend to be. That does not, however, make encounters like this one more acceptable.

Ask this question: How can you make sure people in your company "get it" and delight your customers? Going that extra mile can transform your entire journey into one of gratifying success.

Although "perfect" leaders don't exist, the best of them have a high degree of self-knowledge. They understand their capabilities and capacities. They know what they know and what they don't. They strive to learn and grow while viewing their development as "permanently unfinished business."

YOUR LEADERSHIP CHECKLIST: HOW DO YOU FARE?

Although "perfect" leaders don't exist, the best of them have a high degree of self-knowledge. They understand their capabilities and capacities. They know what they know and what they don't. They strive to learn and grow while viewing their development as "permanently unfinished business."

Consider your actions in relation to the qualities using the following checklist I developed. Today's tough-minded leaders:

- Have strong business orientation and understanding as they:
    - exhibit outstanding acumen and judgment.
    - naturally think of the needs of stakeholders.
    - achieve planned results and never make excuses.
    - have a clear understanding of the anatomy and competitive dynamics of their business.
    - focus on the most critical areas while balancing short- and long-term priorities across constituencies.
    - understand the principles of value creation.

- Assume accountability, initiative, and leadership as they:
  - exhibit a strong desire to lead others.
  - take the lead, even in the absence of formal authority.
  - keep apprised of the important operating level details of their organization without impairing empowerment.
  - assert themselves without being overwhelming.
  - build a competitive team focused on creating value, not bureaucracy.
  - create a merit-based (not politically driven) workplace.
  - raise performance expectations continually.
  - deliver on all commitments made.
  - maintain objectivity, differentiating facts from intuition.
  - identify and prevent potential problems.
  - accept and learn from personal defeats.
  - cut their losses and move on.
- Energize teams as they:
  - align their teams to achieve organizational and team goals, not protect personal interests and/or prerogatives.
  - facilitate conflict resolution and genuine communication.
  - cultivate loyalty and trust without expecting fealty; understand the difference.
  - really listen.
  - provide feedback that's constructive and in real time.
  - coach and counsel in a productive manner, helping people discover and achieve their potential.

- Transform their organizations as they:
    - have clear vision and the courage to not only run but change their organizations.
    - have a raging impatience with the status quo.
    - create consensus around change initiatives, recognizing that giving people a say doesn't necessarily mean giving them a vote.
    - experiment and challenge their own thinking.
    - ask penetrating questions that reframe perspectives and undermine preconceptions.
    - maintain flexibility while remaining riveted on their mission and goals.
- Use superior judgment and decisive action regarding people as they:
    - select and profile them objectively.
    - recruit and train them adeptly.
    - relish hiring and promoting high achievers.
    - promote associates based on merit, "leapfrogging" some if appropriate.
    - evaluate people's performance in a tough-minded fashion.
- Embody curiosity and superior thinking as they:
    - examine issues multi-dimensionally.
    - learn about global issues related to their own industry, organization, and the world overall.
    - perceive the patterns of external change and integrate them into their own thinking.
    - maintain curiosity and open-mindedness.

  - use personal time to "give back" to their communities.
- Display emotional intelligence as they:
  - are self-confident but self-deprecating.
  - have a realistic assessment of themselves.
  - control or redirect disruptive/destructive impulses.
  - have the capacity to suspend judgment, to think before acting.
  - understand the impact that their moods, emotions, and actions have on others.
  - understand the distinctive emotional make-up of others and can skillfully anticipate their reactions.
  - build rapport.
- Accept the responsibility to demonstrate solid character as they:
  - overcome fear (courage).
  - do what needs to be done, when it needs to be done, the way it needs to be done, every time (discipline).
  - delay gratification, doing the hard work first.
  - keep all commitments, regardless of the size or type.
  - insist on truth in relationships (that includes the belief that truth-telling is more important than peace-keeping and that the well-being and success of other people are more important than their comfort).
  - crash through quitting points (endurance, persistence, perseverance).
  - see situations and solutions beyond the obvious.

- accept consequences for the results of their actions and decisions.

Can you identify specific decisions you've made and actions you've taken that exemplify these traits? Remember, tough-minded leadership is not philosophical abstraction or textbook grandiosity. It only exists in the "doing."

About Rand Golletz

For three decades, Rand Golletz has obsessively helped organizations—and those who lead them—to succeed. He understands what it takes because he's created success throughout his own career.

The youngest officer in a Fortune 500 company, Rand led its distribution and sales management functions. As senior vice president and chief marketing officer of a Fortune 100 company, Rand was responsible for market research, sales development, brand development, marketing communications, and planning and distribution management.

Rand has served as director and practice leader for a "Big 5" strategy consulting practice as well as COO and CEO of two multi-hundred-million-dollar financial services companies.

Today, Rand heads Rand Golletz Performance Systems, a firm specializing in leadership development, executive coaching, and consulting. He works with senior corporate leaders and business owners on:

- strategy creation and implementation
- team effectiveness and execution
- interpersonal effectiveness
- brand building
- sales management

No one knows better than Rand what it takes to transform hard-headed executives into tough-minded leaders. He helps them unlock the secrets of personal accountability, promote critical thinking, and develop and sustain profitable business relationships.

For more information about Rand Golletz Performance Systems, visit www.RandGolletz.com.

Recommended Reading

During the last 25 years, I've read hundreds of business and personal development books. Those noted here represent the "best of the best of the best." I highly recommend them.

Business Books

Allen, David. *Getting Things Done: The Art of Stress-Free Productivity*. Penguin, 2002.

Bossidy, Larry, Charles Burck, and Ram Charan. *Execution: The Discipline of Getting Things Done.* Crown Business, 2002.

Charan, Ram. *Know-How: The 8 Skills That Separate People Who Perform from Those Who Don't.* Crown Business, 2008.

Deming, W. Edwards. *Out of the Crisis.* The MIT Press, 2000.

DePree, Max. *Leadership Is an Art*. Broadway Business, 2004.

Drucker, Peter. *Management.* Rev. ed. with Foreword by Jim Collins. HarperBusiness, 2008.

Drucker, Peter. *The Effective Executive: The Definitive Guide to Getting the Right Things Done*. Harper Paperbacks, 2006.

Gerber, Michael. *E-Myth Mastery: The Seven Essential Disciplines for Building a World Class Company.* Harper Paperbacks, 2007.

McGregor, Douglas. *The Human Side of Enterprise.* Annotated ed., McGraw-Hill, 2005.

Peters, Thomas J., and Robert H. Waterman. *In Search of Excellence.* Harper Paperbacks, 2004.

Porter, Michael E. *Competitive Advantage: Creating and Sustaining Superior Performance.* Free Press, 1998.

Senge, Peter M. *The Fifth Discipline: The Art & Practice of the Learning Organization.* Broadway Business, 2006.

Tichy, Noel M. *The Leadership Engine: Building Leaders at Every Level.* Pritchett, LP, 2007.

Personal Development Books

Covey, Stephen R. *The 7 Habits of Highly Effective People.* Free Press, revised, 2004.

Canfield, Jack, and Janet Switzer. *The Success Principles: How to Get from Where You Are to Where You Want to Be.* Harper Paperbacks, 2006.

Hill, Napoleon. *Think and Grow Rich.* Orig. version, restored and revised. Aventine Press, 2004.

Maltz, Maxwell. *Psycho-Cybernetics: A New Way to Get More Living Out of Life.* Pocket, 1989. (See also Maxwell Maltz. *The New Psycho-Cybernetics.* Edited and updated by Dan S. Kennedy and the Psycho-Cybernetics Foundation, Inc., Prentice Hall, 2002.)

Peck, M. Scott. *The Road Less Traveled: A New Psychology of Love, Traditional Values and Spiritual Growth.* 25th Anniv. ed., Touchstone, 2003.

Robbins, Anthony. *Unlimited Power: The New Science of Personal Achievement.* Free Press, 1997.

Tracy, Brian. *Maximum Achievement: Strategies and Skills That Will Unlock Your Hidden Powers to Succeed.* Simon & Schuster, 1995.

PLUS any of the audio or video programs created by the late, great Jim Rohn.

Be sure to subscribe to my award-winning newsletter, "The Real Deal," at www.RandGolletz.com.